MEALS·IN·A·MUFFIN

MEALS·IN·A·MUFFIN

Beverly Worrell and Alice Chapin

Illustrations by
Michelle Burchard

HPBooks

HPBooks
Published by The Berkley Publishing Group
200 Madison Avenue
New York, NY 10016

First edition: March 1995

Published simultaneously in Canada.

Library of Congress Cataloging-in-Publication Data

Worrell, Beverly
    Meals-in-a-muffin / Beverly Worrell and Alice Chapin. —1st ed.
        p.   cm.
    Includes index.
    ISBN 1-55788-200-2 (paper : alk.)
    1. Muffins. 2. Entrées (Cookery) I. Chapin, Alice. II. Title.
TX770.M83W67 1995
641.8'15—dc20   94-29861
                                                                            CIP

Printed in the United States of America

10 9 8 7 6 5 4 3 2 1

Notice: The information printed in this book is true and
complete to the best of our knowledge. All recommendations
are made without any guarantees on the part of the author or
the publisher. The author and publisher disclaim all liability
in connection with the use of this information.

This book is printed on acid-free paper

∞

Acknowledgments

Our thanks to Rubbermaid, Corning Ware, and Chicago Cutlery for use of their products in our home test kitchens.

Contents

MEALS·IN·A·MUFFIN

Introduction

Finger-lickin' meals-in-one baked in regular or giant muffin cups? Why didn't someone think of it before? Here's an entirely new and incredibly easy way of cooking and baking that blends right in with the busy schedules of today's cooks. The recipes for these savory creations are from the exclusive files of Atlanta's Beverly Worrell.

These unique little main-dish muffin masterpieces are endlessly versatile—elegant enough to serve as entrees to persnickety guests at formal dinners or perfectly portable to go with you to work or to microwave for potluck. They can also add a lot of love and cheer to lunchboxes. Just stand aside and watch these delicious and nutritious treats disappear, then wait for the raves!

How do these sound for dinner tonight—Yams & Ham Muffins, Sunday Dinner Muffins featuring chicken and dressing, Italian Spaghetti Muffins, Florida Chili Cornmeal Muffins or Reuben Muffins with corned beef and sauerkraut? Food editors have raved about Bev's Muffins de Soul, a golden delicious cornmeal creation loaded with collard greens and smoked ham. What a way to use leftovers! We have even included other "complete meal" recipes that can be eaten out of hand, meat pockets, stromboli, empanadas, and a few entrees like Mexican Pizza Puffins and Baked Shrimp Crepes.

If you love a warm and succulent plateful of regular down-home muffins to perfectly complete a soup and salad meal or a sumptuous dinner, there are plenty of those recipes, too. Bev shares her unique versions of all-time favorites like old-fashioned blueberry, hearty whole-grain, or bran muffins as well as delectable cobbler muffins bursting with fresh apples or berries.

Her yummy recipes for dessert muffins are here, too—Chocolate Brownie Muffins, Coconut Pecan Muffins, and surprise-filled Tangy Lemon Pudding Muffins. A bountiful basketful of any of these will serve as a sunny and cordial welcome to new neighbors or as a heartfelt thank-you to a friend for a special favor. They are great for on-the-go snacks, too. Best of all, most can be made in double batches and frozen.

Beverly Worrell manages her own Puffin' Muffin shops around Atlanta and is now much in demand by caterers for banquets and conferences. Alice Chapin is a long-time baking hobbyist and best-selling author. The delectable recipes in this book have been double tested by Bev herself. They won't break your budget, either, since most ingredients are found in regular supermarkets and there is no need for unusual expensive kitchen equipment. Be sure to take special note of the exclusive list of helps and hints for better baking.

Enjoy!

Baking Hints
from Puffin' Muffin

• If margarine is used, select a stick product because those labeled "spreads" are softer and not suitable for baking.

• Muffins will taste and look better if muffin paper liners are not used to line cups except as directed, usually in dessert muffins with fruit and larger amounts of sugar. When removed, liners often pull off the tasty outside crust.

• For less cleanup, flour-based spray can be used. We recommend Baker's Joy. Spray between the cups too in case muffins rise up over the sides. Pans with nonstick finish should be greased, too.

• Meals in a muffin are extra tasty if pans are greased with leftover bacon drippings.

• If you lack batter to fill all cups, fill the empty ones with water to protect the pan and to ensure even baking.

• Purposely filling one cup in each pan with water helps keep muffin tops moist or from baking too brown.

• An ice cream scoop makes a great muffin batter scoop. Or, use a one-quarter cup measure with a handle.

• To ensure lighter, fluffier muffins, use room temperature ingredients and sift flour and baking powder.

• Use only double-acting baking powder so leavening will occur both at room temperature and during baking. Make sure baking powder and baking soda are mixed evenly with other dry ingredients to avoid holes in the muffins and an off flavor.

• Do not make flour substitutions. Differing amounts of whole-wheat or all-purpose flour will be required. Self-rising flour is inappropriate.

- In doubling a recipe, baking powder, salt, spices, and flavoring are *not* doubled proportionately. Using three-quarters of these ingredients will usually be sufficient.

- For even texture, never overmix muffin batter. Light folding or hand stirring (about 15 strokes) with a spoon or spatula is usually sufficient unless otherwise indicated. Nuts and fruits should be stirred in with only two or three strokes. Overmixed batter produces tough, dry muffins or air tunnels. Cornmeal batter can be mixed more thoroughly without risk.

- Muffin batters vary: some are thicker than others. Batter will often appear lumpy in the bowl. Lumps usually disappear during baking.

- To keep berries and other fruit from sinking to the bottom, either add them to the dry ingredients or flour them lightly before stirring them into batter.

- Recipes that yield 12 regular-size muffins will make only 4 when baked in giant muffin cups. The best oversized pans we found are manufactured by ROWOCO.

- Unless otherwise directed, most standard muffins (those used to replace breads and rolls) should be cooled in baking pans for only about 5 minutes, then loosened with a kitchen spatula before removal. If left to cool too long in pans, these muffins often get sticky-moist on bottoms. Cobbler muffins will be easier to remove if allowed to remain in cups 10 minutes before removing.

- Test for doneness of standard muffins by checking the tops. They should feel springy to the touch. Or, insert a wooden pick in centers of muffins: they are done when the pick comes out clean.

- Muffins look beautiful stored in a glass jar. A loose-fitting cover is essential so tops will not become sticky. Room temperature is best for storage.

- IMPORTANT: Muffins containing cheese, meat, or other perishables must be refrigerated.

- Pack cooled muffins in an airtight plastic container. Freeze four to eight weeks.

- To defrost regular-size muffins, set them on a paper towel in a microwave at highest setting for 30 to 60 seconds. Frozen muffins can also be wrapped loosely in foil and placed in a *conventional* oven for about 20 minutes at 375°F (190°C).

- For busy cooks: Measure and stir together dry ingredients for a batch of your favorite muffins and store in a covered jar for later use. Add liquid ingredients when you are ready to bake.

- Most regular muffin recipes are very forgiving. They usually make plenty of allowance for new-cook error. Even a child can easily stir up a savory batch.

- In these recipes, large eggs are to be used unless otherwise indicated.

Meals in Muffins

A hot, all-in-one meal baked in a muffin cup is possibly the most sensational and unique new cooking idea ever. No more planning a main dish plus vegetable plus bread. Just wait until you try some of these interesting new combinations using your favorite veggies, cheeses, sausage, seafood, and even baked beans, pasta, chicken and dressing, and more.

Each muffin meal is a savory supper or lunch, perfect for family or even unexpected guests. These scrumptious recipes are truly for kitchen show-offs just like you.

Broccoli & Cheese Muffins

Rich in vitamins with the wonderful flavor of broccoli and cheese.

2 cups cooked chopped broccoli
1 cup shredded Cheddar cheese (4 ounces)
2 tablespoons margarine
1/2 cup chopped onions
1 cup chopped mushrooms
1/4 cup plus 2 tablespoons all-purpose flour
1/2 cup water
1 teaspoon salt
1/2 teaspoon baking powder
1 teaspoon dried leaf oregano, crushed
1/4 teaspoon pepper
2 eggs

Preheat oven to 400°F (205°C). Grease 4 giant muffin cups. In a medium-size bowl, stir together broccoli and cheese. Set aside.

In a medium-size nonstick skillet, melt margarine. Add onions and mushrooms and cook over medium heat 5 minutes. Stir in the 2 tablespoons flour. Gradually stir in water and simmer, stirring, until sauce thickens.

In a small bowl, stir together the 1/4 cup flour, salt, baking powder, oregano, and pepper. Set aside. In a large bowl, beat eggs well with a whisk, then gradually whisk in flour-oregano mixture. Stir in broccoli-cheese mixture and mushroom mixture. Fill muffin cups two-thirds full.

Bake 30 minutes or until light golden brown. Allow to cool in pan 5 minutes. Makes 4 giant muffins.

Easy Baked-Bean Muffins

A great vegetarian meal or serve as a side dish.

2 (16-oz.) cans pork and beans, undrained
1/4 cup finely chopped onion
1/2 cup chopped celery
1 egg, well beaten
1 cup soft bread crumbs
1 teaspoon Worcestershire sauce
3/4 teaspoon salt
1/8 teaspoon red (cayenne) pepper
2 tablespoons light brown sugar
2 tablespoons ketchup
1 tablespoon prepared mustard

Preheat oven to 350°F (175°C). Heavily grease 4 giant muffin cups. In a large bowl, mash beans.

Stir in onion, celery, egg, bread crumbs, Worcestershire sauce, salt, cayenne, brown sugar, ketchup, and mustard. Blend well. Fill each muffin cup to the top.

Bake 60 to 65 minutes or until muffins pull away from sides of cups. Allow to cool in pan 5 minutes. Cover with a plate and invert pan to dislodge muffins. Makes 4 giant muffins.

Reuben Muffins

Serve with mustard for that real deli experience right at home.

1 teaspoon baking soda
2 cups buttermilk
3-1/2 cups all-purpose flour
2 teaspoons sugar
2 teaspoons baking powder
1 teaspoon salt
2 eggs, lightly beaten
1/3 cup vegetable oil
1 (18-oz.) can sauerkraut, well drained
1-1/2 cups finely chopped canned corned beef
4 ounces Swiss cheese cut into 1/2-inch cubes

Preheat oven to 350°F (175°C). Grease 9 giant muffin cups. In a small bowl, stir baking soda into buttermilk. In a large bowl, stir together flour, sugar, baking powder, and salt.

In a medium-size bowl, beat together eggs and oil with a whisk. Stir in the buttermilk mixture. Fold into flour mixture just until dry ingredients are moistened. Gently fold in sauerkraut, corned beef, and cheese cubes. Fill muffin cups three-quarters full.

Bake 45 to 50 minutes or until golden brown. Allow to cool in pan 5 minutes. Makes 9 giant muffins.

Cheeseburger Muffins

A muffin with a meat crust filled with cheese and mushrooms makes a super entree.

1 pound lean ground beef
3/4 cup evaporated milk
1/2 cup corn flake cereal crumbs
1 teaspoon garlic salt
1 (6-oz.) can tomato paste
1-2/3 cups shredded mozzarella cheese (about 7 ounces)
2 tablespoons grated Parmesan cheese plus extra for serving (optional)
1 (4-oz.) can sliced mushrooms, drained
1/2 teaspoon dried leaf oregano

Preheat oven to 350°F (175°C). Line 5 giant muffin cups with foil; spray foil with nonstick cooking spray. In a medium-size bowl, stir together beef, milk, corn flake crumbs, and garlic salt.

Divide meat mixture into 5 equal balls and place a ball in each muffin cup. Using fingers, press meat across the bottom and up the sides of cups.

Divide and spread tomato paste over meat mixture. Place 1/3 cup mozzarella cheese in center of each meat-lined cup. Sprinkle Parmesan cheese over mozzarella cheese. Top with mushrooms and oregano.

Bake 20 to 25 minutes or until lightly browned. Gently remove muffins from cups and place on paper towels to drain. Sprinkle with additional Parmesan cheese when serving, if desired. Makes 5 giant muffins.

Easiest Cheesiest Blintz Muffins

These rich muffins make elegant additions to a brunch menu.

1/2 cup margarine, softened
1/4 cup sugar
2 eggs
3/4 cup milk
1-1/4 cups all-purpose flour
1 teaspoon baking powder
Cheese filling (see below)
Any fruit preserves for topping

Cheese Filling:

8 ounces cottage cheese, drained
8 ounces cream cheese, softened
1 egg
2 tablespoons sugar
1-1/2 teaspoons fresh lemon juice

Preheat oven to 400°F (205°C). Grease 15 (2-3/4-inch) muffin cups. In a large bowl, using mixer at high speed, beat together margarine, sugar, and eggs. Beat in milk.

In a small bowl, stir together flour and baking powder. Stir flour mixture into margarine mixture, stirring just to moisten dry ingredients. Prepare filling.

Using half the batter, spoon 1 tablespoon into bottom of each muffin cup. Divide and spoon filling into muffin cups, then top with remaining batter.

Bake 30 minutes or until light golden brown. Allow to cool in pan 5 minutes. Carefully turn out of muffin cups. Top warm muffins with enough fruit preserves to suit your taste. Makes 15 (2-3/4-inch) muffins.

Cheese Filling:

In a medium-size bowl, using mixer at medium speed, beat together cottage cheese, cream cheese, egg, sugar, and lemon juice.

Italian Spaghetti Muffins

A brand new twist on spaghetti. Delicious!

6 ounces spaghetti, cooked and drained (about 3 cups)
3 tablespoons margarine, melted
1/3 cup grated Parmesan cheese
2 eggs, well beaten
1 cup cottage cheese, drained
1 pound ground turkey or beef
3/4 cup chopped onion
1/4 cup chopped green bell pepper
1 (8-oz.) can stewed tomatoes
1 (6-oz.) can tomato paste
1 teaspoon sugar
1-1/2 teaspoons dried leaf oregano, crushed
1/2 teaspoon garlic salt
1 cup shredded mozzarella cheese (4 ounces)

Preheat oven to 350°F (175°C). Line 6 giant muffin cups with foil; spray foil with nonstick cooking spray. In a large bowl, stir together warm spaghetti and margarine. Add Parmesan cheese and eggs, then toss with a fork to combine.

Divide spaghetti mixture and spoon into bottom of muffin cups forming a nest. Spread cottage cheese over spaghetti (about 1-1/2 tablespoons per muffin). Set aside.

In a large skillet, cook ground turkey or beef, onion, and bell pepper until vegetables are tender, stirring to break up meat. Drain off excess fat. Stir in tomatoes, tomato paste, sugar, oregano, and garlic salt. Cook over medium heat 5 minutes.

Spoon meat mixture into muffin cups, filling each to the top. Sprinkle mozzarella cheese on top.

Bake 30 to 35 minutes or until cheese is light brown. Use a spatula to remove muffins. Makes 6 giant muffins.

Ham & Cheese Brunch Muffins

Great egg dish for brunch or lunch.

1-1/2 cups finely chopped ham
1 cup plain yogurt
1/4 cup shredded Swiss cheese (1 ounce)
1/4 cup saltine cracker crumbs (8 crackers)
2 tablespoons margarine, melted
6 eggs

Preheat oven to 375°F (175°C). Grease 12 (2-3/4-inch) muffin cups. In a large bowl, stir together ham, yogurt, cheese, cracker crumbs, and margarine.

In a medium-size bowl, beat eggs until thick and frothy. Fold eggs into yogurt mixture. Fill muffin cups three-quarters full.

Bake 20 to 25 minutes or until lightly browned. Allow to cool in pan 5 minutes. Loosen muffins with a spatula. Makes 12 (2-3/4-inch) muffins.

Sausage Pizza Muffins

The color is a luscious Napoli red.

8 ounces Italian sausage (2 sausages), removed from casings
2 cups all-purpose flour
1 tablespoon baking powder
1/4 teaspoon salt
1/8 teaspoon pepper
1/2 teaspoon dried leaf oregano, crushed
1/3 cup grated Parmesan cheese
1 egg, lightly beaten
1 (14-oz.) jar pizza sauce
About 2 tablespoons olive oil
1/4 cup shredded mozzarella cheese (1 ounce)

Preheat oven to 400°F (175°C). Grease 12 (2-3/4-inch) muffin cups. In a large skillet, crumble sausage and cook over medium heat, stirring occasionally until sausage is brown. Remove sausage from skillet with a slotted spoon and drain on paper towels. Reserve drippings and allow to cool in skillet.

In a large bowl, stir together flour, baking powder, salt, pepper, oregano, and Parmesan cheese.

In a medium-size bowl, beat together egg and pizza sauce with a whisk. Stir enough olive oil into cooled sausage drippings in skillet to make 3 tablespoons and add to pizza sauce mixture.

Add cooked sausage to flour mixture and toss with a fork to combine. Fold in pizza sauce mixture. Batter will be thick and red in color. Fill muffin cups three-quarters full. Sprinkle with mozzarella cheese.

Bake 20 minutes or until muffins spring back when lightly pressed. Allow to cool in pan 5 minutes. Makes 12 (2-3/4-inch) muffins.

Salmon Muffins

Seafood lovers will especially enjoy this unusual way to serve salmon.

1 (1-lb.) can salmon
1 (10-1/2-oz.) can cream of celery soup
1-1/4 cups fine bread crumbs
3 eggs, well beaten
1/2 cup chopped onion
1 tablespoon fresh lemon juice

Preheat oven to 350°F (175°C). Heavily grease 4 giant muffin cups. In a large bowl, stir together liquid from salmon and soup, then stir in bread crumbs, eggs, onion, and lemon juice.

Remove and discard skin and bones from salmon. Flake salmon and stir into bread crumb mixture. Blend well. Fill muffin cups to top.

Bake 60 minutes or until muffins are golden brown and begin to pull away from sides. Allow to cool in pan 10 minutes before removing with a spatula. Makes 4 giant muffins.

Upside-Down Baked Noodle Muffins

To freeze, just fold up the foil around each muffin.

8 ounces medium-width noodles, cooked and cooled
1/2 cup grated Parmesan cheese
3 eggs, well beaten
2 tablespoons margarine, melted and cooled
2 tablespoons chopped parsley
1/4 teaspoon dried garlic flakes
8 ounces Italian sausage (2 sausages), removed from casings
1/4 cup finely chopped onion
1 (16-oz.) can stewed tomatoes
1 teaspoon dried leaf oregano, crushed
1 teaspoon sugar
1/2 cup shredded mozzarella cheese (2 ounces)

Preheat oven to 350°F (175°C). Line 6 giant muffin cups with foil; spray foil with nonstick cooking spray. In a large bowl, add noodles, 1/4 cup of the Parmesan cheese, eggs, margarine, parsley, and garlic flakes, then toss with a fork to combine. Set aside.

In a large skillet, crumble sausage and cook over medium heat until brown, stirring to break up meat. Drain off excess fat. Add onion and cook over medium heat 5 minutes or until onion is tender. Stir in tomatoes, oregano, and sugar. Bring to a boil, reduce heat, then cover and simmer 20 minutes. Remove from heat and stir in mozzarella cheese.

Divide tomato mixture among muffin cups. Top tomato mixture with noodle mixture (about 3/4 cup for each).

Bake 15 minutes. Allow to cool in pan 5 minutes, then invert pan on platter. Sprinkle with remaining Parmesan cheese when served. Makes 6 giant muffins.

Cheesy Bacon Muffins

For a milder flavor, use Longhorn or Colby cheese.

2 cups all-purpose flour
1 tablespoon baking powder
1/2 teaspoon salt
1/4 teaspoon red (cayenne) pepper
1/4 cup nonfat dried milk powder
1 cup shredded Cheddar cheese (4 ounces)
2 eggs
1/2 cup vegetable oil
1 cup water
10 strips regular or turkey bacon, well cooked and crumbled

Preheat oven to 400°F (205°C). Grease 12 (2-3/4-inch) muffin cups. In a large bowl, stir together flour, baking powder, salt, cayenne, and dried milk. Stir in shredded cheese.

In a small bowl, beat together eggs, vegetable oil, and water with a whisk. Add egg mixture to flour mixture and stir just until dry ingredients are moistened. Fold in crumbled bacon. Fill muffin cups two-thirds full.

Bake 20 minutes or until light golden brown. Allow to cool in pan 5 minutes. Makes 12 (2-3/4-inch) muffins.

Hash Brown Potato Muffins

A great side dish or entree—simply savory.

1 (32-oz.) package frozen hash brown potatoes, partially thawed
1/2 cup margarine, melted
2 cups shredded Cheddar cheese (8 ounces)
1-1/4 cups finely chopped onions
2 cups sour cream
1 (10-1/2-oz.) can condensed cream of chicken soup
1/2 teaspoon garlic salt

Preheat oven to 350°F (175°C). Heavily grease 8 giant muffin cups. In a large bowl, break up potatoes.
Stir in margarine, cheese, onions, sour cream, soup, and garlic salt. Fill muffin cups to top.
Bake 60 minutes or until golden brown. Allow to cool 10 minutes, then use spatula to remove muffins from cups. Makes 8 giant muffins.

Sunday Dinner Muffins

This all-in-one chicken dinner with dressing can be eaten out of hand. It rates rave reviews!

1-1/2 pounds boneless chicken breast
1-3/4 teaspoons salt
2 (7/8-oz.) packages turkey gravy mix
4 chicken bouillon cubes, crushed
2 cups very hot water
1/4 cup margarine
1 cup chopped celery
1 cup chopped onion
4 cups fresh bread crumbs
2 cups cornbread crumbs
1 tablespoon poultry seasoning
1/2 teaspoon pepper
1/4 cup chopped parsley
1 (6-1/2-oz.) can evaporated milk
2 eggs, well beaten

Preheat oven to 350°F (175°C). Grease 6 giant muffin cups. Place chicken in a microwave-safe dish. Sprinkle chicken with 3/4 teaspoon of the salt and microwave on high 20 minutes or until almost done. Cut chicken breasts into 24 small pieces. Set aside. Follow directions on package to make gravy. Place chicken pieces in gravy.

In a small bowl, dissolve bouillon cubes in hot water. Set aside. In a large skillet, melt margarine. Add celery and onion and cook over low heat 5 minutes or until vegetables are tender. Stir in bouillon. Allow to cool.

In a large bowl, stir together bread crumbs, cornbread crumbs, poultry seasoning, pepper, parsley, and remaining 1 teaspoon salt, then stir in milk and eggs until well blended. Stir in cooled vegetable-bouillon mixture.

Using half the mixture, cover the bottom of each muffin cup. Remove chicken pieces from gravy and arrange atop dressing in muffin cups, pressing downward slightly. Cover chicken with remaining dressing using a spatula around sides of muffin cup to make room for the top layer and to seal with the bottom dressing.

Bake 40 minutes. Use spatula to remove muffins from cups. Allow to cool in pan 5 minutes. Heat remaining gravy to pour over muffins when serving. Makes 6 giant muffins.

Tamale Cheese Muffins

Prefer HOT tamales? Sprinkle jalapeño chiles on top as a garnish.

Beef Filling (see below)
1-1/4 cups cornmeal
4-1/2 cups milk
1-1/2 tablespoons margarine
1-1/2 teaspoons salt
3 eggs, well beaten
2-1/2 cups shredded Cheddar cheese (10 ounces)

Beef Filling:

1 pound lean ground beef
1 medium onion, chopped
1 cup sliced mushrooms
1 (17-oz.) can stewed tomatoes
1 (15-oz.) can whole-kernel corn
1/4 cup chopped green bell pepper
1 tablespoon chili powder
1/2 teaspoon dried minced garlic
1 teaspoon salt
1 teaspoon sugar
1/2 cup sliced pitted ripe olives

Preheat oven to 350°F (175°C). Grease 8 giant muffin cups. Prepare filling. In a small bowl, stir together cornmeal and 1 cup milk. Set aside.

In a large saucepan, stir together remaining milk, margarine, and salt. Bring to a boil over medium heat. Gradually stir in cornmeal mixture with a whisk. Stir constantly until mixture thickens. Simmer 15 minutes over low heat, stirring occasionally. Stir in eggs, then 1-1/2 cups of the cheese. Remove from heat and continue stirring until cheese melts.

Spoon cornmeal batter equally into muffin cups, reserving 1 cup. Divide meat mixture among the 8 muffin cups. Top with a heaping tablespoon of cornmeal batter and sprinkle with remaining 1 cup cheese. Bake 50 minutes or until edges are brown and cheese is bubbly. Allow to cool in pan 10 minutes before removing with spatula. Makes 8 giant muffins.

Beef Filling:

In a large skillet over medium heat, crumble ground beef with onion and cook 5 minutes or until beef loses color, stirring occasionally to break up meat. Stir in mushrooms, tomatoes, corn, bell pepper, chili powder, dried garlic, salt, and sugar. Cover and simmer 45 minutes over low heat. Add olives and simmer 15 minutes.

Broccoli & Cheddar Knish Muffins

So unusually delicious and hearty!

2 cups all-purpose flour
1 teaspoon powdered sugar
2/3 cup margarine, chilled
2 eggs
1 tablespoon white wine vinegar

Potato Filling:

3 cups mashed cooked potatoes
1-1/2 teaspoon salt
1/8 cup olive oil
1 egg, well beaten
3/4 cup finely chopped onion
1 cup finely chopped broccoli (flowerets only)
1/2 cup shredded Cheddar cheese (2 ounces)

Preheat oven to 350°F (175°C). Grease 4 giant muffin cups. Prepare pastry: In a medium-size bowl, stir together flour and sugar. Using a pastry blender, cut in margarine until mixture resembles coarse cornmeal.

Beat 1 egg with vinegar and stir into dry ingredients. Knead dough with lightly floured hands until dry ingredients are dampened enough to form a ball. Cover and refrigerate.

Prepare filling. Roll out refrigerated dough to 1/8-inch thickness. Cut into four equal rectangular pieces, then line muffin cups, allowing extra dough to hang over edges. Spoon filling into pastry. Fold ends of pastry over top of filling. Beat remaining egg with 1 tablespoon water and brush over pastry. Bake 60 minutes or until golden brown. Allow to cool in pan 5 minutes. Makes 4 giant muffins.

Potato Filling:

In a large bowl stir together mashed potatoes, salt, olive oil, egg, onion, broccoli, and cheese. Blend well.

Broccoli, Rice & Cheese Muffins

Quick and easy to make.

1 (1-lb.) package frozen chopped broccoli
1/4 cup chopped onion
1 (8-oz.) jar Cheez Whiz
2 cups cooked rice (see Note, page 39)
1 (10-3/4-oz.) can condensed cream of celery soup
1 cup fine bread crumbs
1 tablespoon melted margarine

Preheat oven to 350°F (175°C). Grease 4 giant muffin cups. In a large microwave-safe bowl, microwave frozen broccoli on HIGH 8 to 10 minutes. Drain off liquid. Stir in onion.

Remove lid from cheese jar and microwave on MEDIUM 3 to 5 minutes or until cheese is melted. Stir cheese, rice, and soup into broccoli mixture. Blend well. Divide mixture among the muffin cups. Sprinkle with bread crumbs and drizzle margarine over crumbs.

Bake 30 to 35 minutes or until bread crumbs are golden brown. Allow to cool in pan 10 minutes. Use a spatula to remove muffins. Makes 4 giant muffins.

Summer Squash & Onion Muffins

You need only a salad to complete this meal.

3 cups cooked chopped summer squash
3/4 cup chopped onion
2 tablespoons melted margarine, cooled
3 eggs, well beaten
2 cups fresh bread crumbs
1 cup evaporated milk
1 teaspoon salt
1/8 teaspoon pepper

Preheat oven to 350°F (175°C). Heavily grease 6 giant muffin cups. In a large bowl, stir together squash and onion. Set aside.

In a small bowl, beat together margarine and eggs with a whisk. In another large bowl, stir together bread crumbs and evaporated milk, then stir in egg mixture. Fold in squash mixture, salt, and pepper. Divide mixture among muffin cups.

Bake 30 to 45 minutes or until a knife inserted in centers of muffins comes out clean. Do not brown. Allow to cool in pan 5 minutes. Use a spatula to remove muffins. Makes 6 giant muffins.

Italian Spinach Muffins

Mama mia! That's what guests will say about this Old World recipe.

1-1/2 pounds Italian sausage (6 sausages), removed from casings
1 cup chopped onions
3/4 cup chopped red bell pepper
1 (10-oz.) package frozen chopped spinach, thawed and drained well
1 cup all-purpose flour
1/4 cup grated Parmesan cheese
1/2 teaspoon salt
1/4 teaspoon black pepper
1 teaspoon dried leaf basil
8 eggs
2 cups milk
1 cup shredded mozzarella cheese (4 ounces)

Preheat oven to 350°F (175°C). Heavily grease 8 giant muffin cups. Crumble sausage with onions in a large skillet and cook over medium heat until sausage is browned, stirring to break up meat. Remove from skillet and drain on paper towels. Divide sausage equally among muffin cups.

Divide bell peppers into 2 portions and sprinkle half on top of sausage, then add a layer of spinach. Set aside.

In a large bowl, stir together flour, Parmesan cheese, salt, black pepper, and basil. In a medium-size bowl using electric mixer at high speed, beat eggs well, then at low speed, beat in milk. Gradually add egg mixture to flour mixture, stirring constantly until well blended.

Fill each muffin cup with about 3/4 cup batter. Place muffin pan in a jellyroll pan, then pour 1/3 cup water in jellyroll pan. Bake 25 minutes or until a knife inserted into centers of muffins comes out clean. Remove muffins from oven and top with remaining bell pepper and mozzarella cheese. Bake 2 minutes to melt cheese. Allow to cool in pan 5 minutes. Use a spatula to remove muffins from cups. Makes 8 giant muffins.

Puffy Chicken & Peas Muffins

A heavenly hearty meal-in-one.

4 chicken bouillon cubes
2 cups boiling water
3/4 cup plus 2 tablespoons margarine
3 tablespoons all-purpose flour
3/4 cup skim milk
2 eggs
1 tablespoon grated Parmesan cheese
1/3 cup cream cheese, softened
1/4 teaspoon pepper
1/4 teaspoon grated nutmeg
1 tablespoon dried minced onion
4 cups cubed cooked chicken
1 (15-oz.) can green peas, drained
24 sheets frozen phyllo pastry dough, thawed

Preheat oven to 375°F (190°C). Heavily grease 8 giant muffin cups. In a small bowl, crush bouillon cubes in boiling water. Set aside.

In a medium-size saucepan over low heat, melt the 2 tablespoons margarine. Using a whisk, gradually stir in flour. Add bouillon mixture and milk and cook, stirring, until mixture thickens. Remove from heat.

In a small bowl, using electric mixer at high speed, beat eggs well, then with mixer at medium speed, beat in 1 cup of hot flour mixture. Blend well. Whisk egg mixture into remaining flour mixture in saucepan.

Stir in Parmesan and cream cheeses, pepper, nutmeg, onion, chicken, and peas. Return mixture to low heat and continue stirring until cheese melts (about 5 minutes). Remove from heat. Set aside.

Melt remaining margarine in a small saucepan over low heat. Unroll phyllo sheets. Using a pastry brush and working quickly, paint every second sheet with melted margarine. Keep phyllo covered with a slightly damp towel. Make a stack of 12 sheets. Cut stack into 6 (6-inch) squares and line 6 muffin cups. Repeat with remaining phyllo and cut off 2 (6-inch) squares from the second stack to line remaining 2 cups. Divide filling among pastry-lined cups. Cut the rest of the stack into 8 (about 3-inch) squares to top muffins. Tuck down corners. Using a pastry brush, paint tops with melted margarine.

Bake 20 minutes or until golden brown. Allow to cool in pan 5 minutes. Carefully remove from muffin cups. Makes 8 giant muffins.

Note

Phyllo pastry dough dries out quickly if uncovered. Keep all the sheets, except the one you are working on, covered with a slightly damp towel or plastic wrap.

Calico Chicken Muffins

Chicken and dressing in a muffin and ready in minutes.

3 eggs
3/4 cup evaporated milk
1 (6-oz.) package stuffing mix
2 cups cubed, cooked chicken
1 large fresh tomato, cubed
3 tablespoons chopped onion
3 tablespoons chopped mild green chiles

Preheat oven to 350°F (175°C). Heavily grease 4 giant muffin cups. In a large bowl, beat eggs well. Stir in milk, stuffing mix, chicken, tomato, onion, and chiles. Blend well. Divide mixture among muffin cups.

Bake 20 minutes or until golden brown. Allow to cool in pan 5 minutes. Use a spatula to remove muffins. Makes 4 giant muffins.

Turkey Gumbo Muffins

This lunchtime treat is so delicious that you are not going to believe how easy it is to make.

1/2 pound turkey sausage
1-1/4 cups cornmeal
1 cup all-purpose flour
1 tablespoon baking powder
1 tablespoon sugar
1 teaspoon seasoned salt
1 cup milk
2 eggs, well beaten
1/4 cup olive oil
1 teaspoon Worcestershire sauce
1/2 teaspoon hot pepper sauce
2 cups fresh okra, thinly sliced (about 1/2 pound)
1/2 cup chopped onion
1 cup cubed fresh tomato

Preheat oven to 375°F (175°C). Grease 7 giant muffin cups. In a medium-size nonstick skillet, cook sausage over medium heat until browned, stirring to break up meat. Drain off fat and allow to cool.

In a large bowl, stir together cornmeal, flour, baking powder, sugar, and seasoned salt. In a small bowl, stir together milk, eggs, olive oil, Worcestershire sauce, and hot pepper sauce. Add milk mixture to cornmeal mixture, stirring just enough to moisten dry ingredients. Fold in okra, onion, tomato, and sausage. Fill muffin cups two-thirds full.

Bake 30 minutes or until golden brown and muffins spring back when lightly touched. Allow to cool in pan 5 minutes. Makes 7 giant muffins.

Variation

If fresh okra is not available, substitute thawed, frozen sliced okra.

Egg-Nest Spinach Muffins

Good enough for company.

2 (10-oz) packages frozen chopped spinach, thawed and drained
1/2 teaspoon salt
3 tablespoons margarine
3 tablespoons all-purpose flour
1 cup milk
1 cup shredded Cheddar cheese (4 ounces)
4 eggs
Salt and pepper

Preheat oven to 325°F (165°C). Line 4 giant muffin cups with foil; spray foil with nonstick cooking spray. In a medium-size bowl, sprinkle thawed spinach with 1/2 teaspoon salt and toss with a fork. Divide spinach into 4 equal parts (about 1/3 cup tightly packed) and cover the bottom of each muffin cup. Make indentations in the spinach. Set aside.

In a small saucepan over low heat, melt margarine, then gradually stir in flour until smooth. Gradually add milk and cook, stirring constantly with a whisk, until mixture thickens. Stir in cheese and remove from heat. Break 1 egg into each of the spinach indentations. Sprinkle each egg with 1/8 teaspoon each salt and pepper. Divide sauce and cover each egg.

Bake 30 to 35 minutes or until sauce is set and begins to bubble and brown. Allow to cool in pan 5 minutes before serving. Use a spatula to remove muffins. Makes 4 giant muffins.

Hominy Grits & Cheddar Muffins

A full breakfast in a muffin.

1 pound bulk turkey sausage
1/2 cup chopped green bell pepper
1 cup finely chopped onion
1 cup chopped celery
2 cups cooked hominy grits
1 cup mozzarella cheese (4 ounces)

Preheat oven to 325°F (165°C). Grease 6 giant muffin cups. In a large nonstick skillet, crumble sausage and cook over medium heat 10 minutes or until browned, stirring to break up meat. Stir in bell pepper, onion, and celery and cook, covered, over low heat 5 to 10 minutes or until vegetables are tender, stirring occasionally.

In a large bowl, stir together grits, sausage mixture, and cheese. Fill muffin cups to top. Bake 30 to 35 minutes or until muffins are firmly set. Allow to cool in pan. When ready to serve, remove with spatula and reheat in microwave. Makes 6 giant muffins.

Note

For 2 cups cooked grits, cook 1 cup grits according to package directions.

Sausage 'n' Egg Muffins

Send everybody off to school or work with a full breakfast in hand.

3 cups all-purpose flour
3 tablespoons sugar
2-1/2 tablespoons baking powder
1 teaspoon salt
3/4 cup margarine, chilled
6 eggs
2 cups milk
6 large cooked sausage patties
6 eggs
6 slices sharp Cheddar cheese

Preheat oven to 350°F (175°C). Grease 6 giant muffin cups. In a large bowl, stir together flour, sugar, baking powder, and salt. Using a pastry blender, cut in margarine until mixture resembles cornmeal.

In a medium-size bowl, beat 6 eggs well with a whisk, then beat in milk. Add milk mixture to flour mixture and stir just enough to moisten dry ingredients.

Using half the batter, cover bottom of muffin cups. Using a spoon, form a small crater, then break an egg in center of each. Top with a cooked sausage patty and 1 slice of cheese, folded if necessary. Cover with remaining batter, then move a spatula around sides to force top batter together with bottom. Bake 25 to 30 minutes or until golden brown. Allow to cool in pan 5 minutes. Makes 6 giant muffins.

Variation

Substitute 6 softly scrambled eggs with cheese for uncooked eggs. Spoon on top of batter as described above.

Easy Cheesy Egg Muffins

These are similar to a quiche without the crust.

7 eggs
1 cup shredded Cheddar cheese (4 ounces)
2 tablespoons all-purpose flour
1/2 cup skim milk
2 tablespoons margarine, melted and cooled
1 teaspoon prepared mustard
1/2 teaspoon salt
1/4 teaspoon pepper
Paprika

Preheat oven to 325°F (165°C). Heavily grease 8 (2-3/4-inch) muffin cups. In a large bowl, using electric mixer at high speed, beat eggs well. Stir in cheese. Place flour in a small bowl, then gradually beat in milk with a small whisk until smooth. Stir flour mixture into egg mixture. Blend well. Stir in margarine, mustard, salt, and pepper.

Fill each muffin cup with about 1/3 cup batter. Set muffin pan in a jellyroll pan and pour 1/3 cup water into bottom of jellyroll pan. Bake 20 to 25 minutes or until eggs are set. Do not brown. Sprinkle tops with paprika and serve hot. Makes 8 (2-3/4-inch) muffins.

Note

Pour water into empty muffin cups for more even baking.

Muffins de Soul

This muffin filled with collard greens and ham won rave reviews from many food editors. Use the meat from the cooked ham hock as part of the filling.

Greens 'n' Ham Filling (see below)
2 cups all-purpose flour
1 cup cornmeal
2 tablespoons plus 2 teaspoons baking powder
2 tablespoons sugar
1-1/2 teaspoons salt
4 eggs
2 cups milk
2/3 cup vegetable oil

Greens 'n' Ham Filling:

1 large ham hock
2 quarts water
1 bunch fresh collard greens
2 teaspoons salt
3 red chiles with seeds or 2 teaspoons dried crushed chiles
1/2 cup bacon drippings
8 ounces smoked ham, cooked and cut into small (1/2- to 3/4-inch) chunks

Prepare filling. Meanwhile, stir together flour, cornmeal, baking powder, sugar, and salt in a large bowl. In a medium-size bowl, beat eggs well with a whisk. Beat in milk and vegetable oil. Gradually add egg mixture to flour mixture and blend well with a large spoon or electric mixer on low. Set aside 60 minutes.

Preheat oven to 400°F (205°C). Grease 4 giant muffin cups including top edges. Fill cups about three-fourths full. Fill a 1/2 cup measure half-full of cooked greens. Add 2 ounces ham, then more greens to top of measure. Place greens and ham on top of batter in a muffin cup and press down with fingers or spoon to force batter upward until it covers filling in a small mound. Remove excess batter with spatula. Repeat for remaining 3 muffin cups.

Bake 15 minutes, then reduce temperature to 325°F (165°C) and bake 15 minutes more or until golden brown. Allow to cool in pan 5 minutes. Makes 4 giant muffins.

Greens 'n' Ham Filling:

In a large covered pot, boil ham hock in water 45 minutes or until nearly done. Meanwhile wash greens, remove stems, and coarsely chop (you will need 3 cups). Add chopped collard greens and salt to ham hock. Bring to a boil, then cook over low heat 60 minutes or until greens are very tender. Stir in chiles and bacon drippings. Squeeze greens gently so some moisture remains. Any unused collards freeze well.

Veggie Lasagna Muffins

Finally, an easy lasagna recipe. Yes, it is shaped into muffins.

1 large (1/2 pound) yellow summer squash, cubed
1 large (1/2 pound) zucchini, cubed
1 large yellow bell pepper, sliced
1 large red bell pepper, sliced
1 large green bell pepper, sliced
1 pound broccoli flowerets, cut into small pieces
1-1/2 teaspoons dried minced garlic
1-1/2 teaspoons Italian seasoning
1 teaspoon salt
Cheese Mixture (see below)
3/4 pound lasagna noodles (12 noodles)
1 cup shredded part-skim milk mozzarella cheese (4 ounces)

Cheese Mixture:

2 eggs
1 (15-oz.) carton ricotta cheese
1 (16-oz.) carton cottage cheese, drained
2 tablespoons dried leaf basil, crushed
1/4 teaspoon hot pepper sauce
1-1/2 cups shredded part-skim milk mozzarella cheese (6 ounces)

Preheat oven to 400°F (205°C). Line 4 giant muffin cups with foil; spray foil well with nonstick cooking spray. In a large microwave-safe bowl, stir together summer squash, zucchini, bell peppers, and broccoli. Stir in garlic and Italian seasoning. Sprinkle with salt and stir again. Cover and microwave on HIGH 8 minutes. Set aside.

Prepare Cheese Mixture. Stir squash mixture into cheese mixture. Place uncooked lasagna noodles in a plastic bag and break into 1- to 1-1/2-inch pieces. Stir uncooked noodles into squash-cheese mixture. Blend well. Divide mixture among muffin cups. Sprinkle with remaining mozzarella cheese.

Bake 15 minutes, then reduce oven temperature to 300°F (150°C) and bake 30 minutes or until muffins are set. Allow to cool in pan 5 minutes. Makes 8 giant muffins.

Cheese Mixture:

In a large bowl, beat eggs well. Stir in ricotta and cottage cheeses, basil, hot pepper sauce, and mozzarella cheese.

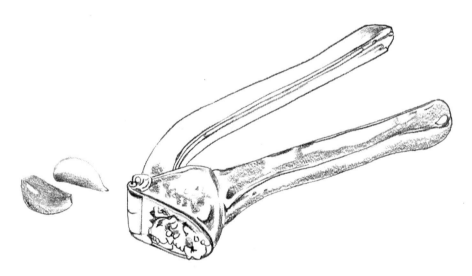

Chili Meat Puffins

Tasty little meat pies are baked in muffin cups.

Chili Filling (see below)
2 cups all-purpose flour
4 teaspoons baking powder
1 teaspoon salt
1 teaspoon sugar
1/2 cup solid vegetable shortening
3/4 cup milk

Chili Filling:

1 pound extra-lean ground beef
1 small onion, chopped
2/3 cup chili sauce
1 teaspoon prepared mustard
1/2 teaspoon salt

Preheat oven to 400°F (205°C). Prepare filling. Grease 4 giant muffin cups. In a large bowl, stir together flour, baking powder, salt, and sugar. Using a pastry blender, cut in shortening until mixture resembles coarse cornmeal. Stir in milk to make a soft dough. On a lightly floured board roll out dough to 1/4-inch thickness and cut into 4 (6-inch) squares.

Line muffin cups with dough squares. Divide filling among dough-lined muffin cups.

Bake 15 minutes, then reduce oven temperature to 350°F (175°C) and bake 10 minutes or until puffins are brown and meat is cooked (filling will be soft). Allow to cool in pan 5 minutes. Makes 4 giant muffins.

Chili Filling:

In a nonstick skillet, stir together ground beef and onion. Cook, stirring constantly, 5 minutes over medium heat. Remove from heat. Stir in chili sauce, mustard, and salt. Blend well. Cool slightly before using.

Yams & Ham Muffins

Pure Southern comfort food.

3 cups mashed cooked sweet potatoes (about 2-1/2 lbs.), cooled
1/8 teaspoon grated orange zest
2 eggs, well beaten
3 tablespoons melted margarine, cooled
3 tablespoons orange juice
1/3 cup packed light brown sugar
1-1/2 cups cubed, cooked smoked ham
1 teaspoon ground cinnamon

Preheat oven to 350°F (175°C). Grease 4 giant muffin cups. In a large bowl, stir together potatoes, orange zest, eggs, margarine, orange juice, and brown sugar. Blend well. Stir in ham.

Divide mixture among muffin cups, then sprinkle tops with cinnamon.

Bake 45 to 50 minutes or until a knife inserted into centers of muffins comes out clean. Allow to cool in pan 10 minutes. Use a spatula to remove muffins from cups. Makes 4 giant muffins.

Creamed Corn Quiche Muffins

Corn muffins without cornmeal.

1/4 cup all-purpose flour
1 teaspoon salt
1/4 teaspoon pepper
1 (15-oz.) can creamed corn
1 tablespoon dried minced onion
3 eggs, well beaten
2 tablespoons margarine, melted and cooled
2 cups milk
1/4 cup dried parsley

Preheat oven to 350°F (175°C). Grease 4 giant muffin cups. In a large bowl, stir together flour, salt, and pepper. Stir in creamed corn and onion.

In a small bowl, beat together eggs and margarine with a whisk, then beat in milk. Add egg mixture to corn mixture and stir to moisten. Lightly stir in parsley. Fill muffin cups to top. Parsley will rise to top.

Bake 60 to 70 minutes or until a knife inserted into centers of muffins comes out clean. Allow to cool in pan 10 minutes. Use a spatula to remove muffins from cups. Makes 4 giant muffins.

Saffron Rice & Ham Muffins

Great with your favorite jam or jelly.

2 eggs
1 cup cooked rice with saffron
1/2 cup nonfat dried milk powder
1-3/4 cups water
3 tablespoons margarine, melted and cooled
2 cups all-purpose flour
5 teaspoons baking powder
1 teaspoon sugar
1/2 teaspoon salt
1-1/2 cups diced cooked ham

Preheat oven to 400°F (205°C). Grease 18 (2-3/4-inch) muffin cups. In a large bowl, beat eggs well. Stir in rice, dried milk, water, and margarine.

In a medium-size bowl, stir together flour, baking powder, sugar, and salt. Add flour mixture to rice mixture and mix well. Stir in ham. Fill muffin cups half full.

Bake 35 minutes or until golden brown and muffins spring back when lightly touched. Allow muffins to cool in pan 5 minutes. Makes 18 (2-3/4-inch) muffins.

Note

One cup uncooked rice makes 2 to 3 cups cooked rice.

Florida Chili Cornmeal Muffins

Your favorite chili is hidden with cheese in the center of each muffin.
Make your favorite chili or use a good canned chili.

2 cups all-purpose flour
2 cups yellow cornmeal
1/2 cup nonfat dried milk powder
2 tablespoons baking powder
1-1/2 teaspoons salt
3 tablespoons sugar
2 large eggs
1/2 cup vegetable oil
2 cups water
4 cups shredded sharp Cheddar cheese (1 pound)
4 cups of your favorite chili, chilled

Preheat oven to 350°F (175°C). Grease 8 giant muffin cups and cup edges. In a large bowl, stir together flour, cornmeal, dried milk, baking powder, salt, and sugar. Set aside.

In a medium-size bowl, beat together eggs and vegetable oil with a whisk, then beat in water. Gradually add egg mixture to cornmeal mixture, stirring well after each addition. Allow batter to stand 1 hour.

Fill muffin cups almost three-quarters full. Push 1/2 cup cheese into center of each muffin, then press in 1/2 cup chili forcing batter up so it covers the cheese and chili completely. Smooth top and remove excess batter with a spatula.

Bake 35 minutes or until golden brown. Allow to cool in pan 5 minutes. Makes 8 giant muffins.

Turkey Vegetable Muffins

Five different veggies fill this muffin, which resembles a meatloaf.

1-1/4 lbs. ground turkey
1 cup diced eggplant
1 medium-size onion, finely chopped
8 to 10 fresh mushrooms, chopped
1 medium-size green bell pepper, chopped
2 medium-size fresh tomatoes, peeled and chopped
2 cups bran flakes cereal
1/3 teaspoon ground sage
1/3 teaspoon dried leaf tarragon
1/3 teaspoon dried leaf oregano
1/2 teaspoon dried minced garlic
1/4 teaspoon black pepper
1 teaspoon salt
2 eggs, well beaten
3/4 cup tomato sauce

Preheat oven to 350°F (175°C). Heavily grease 7 giant muffin cups. In a large bowl, stir together turkey, eggplant, onion, mushrooms, bell pepper, tomatoes, and bran flakes.

In a small bowl, stir together sage, tarragon, oregano, garlic, black pepper, and salt, then beat in the eggs with a whisk. Stir egg mixture into turkey mixture until well blended.

Fill each muffin cup to the top.

Bake 30 minutes. Remove from oven and top with tomato sauce. Return to oven and bake 15 to 20 minutes or until lightly browned. Allow to cool in pan 10 minutes. Makes 7 giant muffins.

Meals in Pockets

Everyone loves these meals in pockets—favorite ingredients like chicken, ground beef, cheese, and sausage enclosed in a delicious, edible wrap. Pockets are sure to be going places, too. They are compact and easily taken along to eat on the go. They can be made in advance and frozen, then popped into lunch bags to be heated (or not) in a microwave, and eaten out of hand.

Yes, these all-in-one meals are hot hits for lunch or supper at home, too. They will fill your kitchen with incredible aromas, and they taste as good as they smell.

Empanadas

A taste of Mexico in a meal-in-one from Bev's Atlanta kitchen.

2-1/2 cups all-purpose flour
1/2 teaspoon salt
1/2 cup margarine, chilled
1/3 cup ice water
Beef & Egg Filling (see below)
1 egg beaten with 1 tablespoon milk for egg wash

Beef & Egg Filling:

1 tablespoon olive oil
1 cup finely chopped onion
1 pound ground beef
1/2 cup raisins
2 teaspoons light brown sugar
1 tablespoon paprika
1/2 teaspoon salt
1 teaspoon cumin
1/8 teaspoon red (cayenne) pepper
1/2 cup chopped pimiento-stuffed olives
2 hard-cooked eggs, finely chopped

In a large bowl, stir together flour and salt. Using a pastry blender, cut in margarine until mixture resembles cornmeal. Sprinkle ice water over mixture, then knead dough with lightly floured hands until ingredients are moistened enough to form a ball. Cover and refrigerate. Prepare filling.

Preheat oven to 350°F (175°C). Grease a large baking sheet. Form dough into 8 smaller balls. On a lightly floured board, roll out each ball into a circle 6 to 7 inches in diameter. Using a pastry brush, brush around edges with water, then divide filling and spoon equally on half of each circle (1/2 to 3/4 cup each).

Fold dough once over filling to make a seam and pinch edges. Prick each with a fork. Place on prepared baking sheet, then using a pastry brush, paint empanadas with egg wash.

Bake 20 minutes or until golden brown. Serve hot. Makes 8 empanadas.

Beef & Egg Filling:

In a nonstick skillet, heat oil, then add onion and ground beef. Cook over medium heat until meat is browned, stirring to break up meat. Pour off fat. Stir in raisins, brown sugar, paprika, salt, cumin, cayenne, olives, and chopped eggs.

Stromboli

A favorite of Bev's Puffin' Muffin shop customers for years.

3 cups all-purpose flour
1 (1/4-oz.) package active dry yeast
1 tablespoon sugar
1-1/2 teaspoons salt
1/2 cup milk
1 cup hot water
1 tablespoon margarine, melted
Meat Filling (see below)
3 tablespoons prepared mustard
2 cups shredded mild Cheddar cheese (8 ounces)
2-1/2 cups shredded mozzarella cheese (10 ounces)
1/2 pound sliced pepperoni
2 tablespoons vegetable oil
1 teaspoon Italian seasoning

Meat Filling:
1/2 pound ground beef
1/2 pound Italian sausage, removed from casings
3/4 cup chopped onion

In the large bowl of an electric mixer, stir together flour, yeast, sugar, and salt using dough paddle on low speed. Set aside.

In a small bowl, stir together milk, water, and melted margarine. Using dough paddle at medium speed, gradually add milk mixture to flour mixture. Increase speed to high and beat dough until it cleans side of bowl and clings to paddle. Knead on lightly floured board 6 minutes.

Cover and let rise in a warm place 1-1/2 hours or until double in size. Cook beef, sausage, and onion for filling. When dough is ready, preheat oven to 350°F (175°C). Grease a large baking sheet. Roll out dough on lightly floured board into a 15″ x 12″ rectangle.

Using a pastry brush, paint dough with half the mustard. Sprinkle half the Cheddar cheese on the center one-third of dough. Sprinkle with half the mozzarella cheese, then add half the pepperoni slices and half the meat filling. Dot with remaining mustard and repeat layers using remaining ingredients. Using a pastry brush, moisten edges of dough with water. Pull both sides of dough over filling to make a seam, then pinch together.

Place Stromboli on baking sheet, seam side down. Paint with vegetable oil and sprinkle with Italian seasoning. Cut 4 small slits on top.

Bake 45 minutes or until golden brown on top and bottom. Slice into 4 pieces and serve hot. Makes 4 hearty servings.

Meat Filling:

In a large skillet, cook ground beef, Italian sausage, and onion over medium heat until browned, stirring to break up meat. Drain well on paper towels.

Cheese-filled Pizza Rolls

Bev says, "This is one of my favorite recipes."

3 cups all-purpose flour
1 (1/4-oz.) package active dry yeast
2 teaspoons sugar
1 teaspoon salt
1-1/2 tablespoons olive oil
1 cup lukewarm water
Pizza Filling (see below)
1/4 cup olive oil
1 tablespoon Italian seasoning
1 egg beaten with 1 tablespoon water for egg wash

Pizza Filling:

1/2 pound Italian sausage (2 sausages)
1 pound cottage or ricotta cheese, drained
2 eggs, well beaten
1/3 cup grated Parmesan cheese
1/2 cup shredded mozzarella cheese (2 ounces)

In the large bowl of an electric mixer, combine flour, yeast, sugar, and salt, using dough paddle on low speed. In a small bowl, beat together olive oil and lukewarm water with a whisk. With mixer on low, gradually add water mixture to flour mixture. Increase speed to high and beat until dough cleans sides of bowl and clings to paddle. Knead 2 minutes on lightly floured board. Cover with a towel and let rise in a warm place 1 hour or until double in size. Prepare filling.

When dough is ready, preheat oven to 325°F (165°C). Grease a large baking sheet. Divide dough into 6 balls. Roll each ball on a lightly floured board to a circle 6 to 7 inches in diameter. Using a pastry brush, paint with olive oil and sprinkle with Italian seasoning. Divide filling and spoon into center of each dough circle. Carefully pull ends together just until they meet (without overlapping), then pinch to form a seam on top. Place pizzas seam side down on baking sheet and prick top with a fork.

In a cup, beat egg and 1 tablespoon water together with a small whisk. Using a pastry brush, paint top and sides with egg wash.

Bake 40 minutes or until golden brown on all sides. Serve hot. Makes 6 pizza rolls.

Pizza Filling:

In a medium-size nonstick skillet, cook sausage over medium heat until browned. Drain off fat and allow to cool. Cut sausage into thin slices. In a large bowl, stir together cottage cheese, eggs, Parmesan cheese, and mozzarella cheese. Stir in sausage.

Baked Shrimp Crepes

The crepes can be made ahead of time and refrigerated, stacked with pieces of waxed paper between them.

1 egg
1 cup all-purpose flour
1 cup water
1/4 teaspoon salt

Filling:

3/4 cup finely chopped snow peas
1 cup finely chopped bean sprouts
1/2 cup finely chopped mushrooms
1/2 pound cooked shrimp, shelled and finely chopped
1/2 cup finely chopped celery
1 medium-size green bell pepper, finely chopped
2 tablespoons soy sauce
1 teaspoon salt

Preheat oven to 400°F (205°C). Grease a large baking sheet. Combine egg, flour, water, and salt in a blender or food processor and process 15 seconds. Spray a nonstick 9-inch skillet with nonstick cooking spray. Heat skillet over medium heat. Pour in just enough batter to cover bottom and cook until firm. Remove from skillet. Repeat with remaining batter.

Prepare filling. Divide filling and spoon equally in the center of crepes. Bring both sides of each crepe toward the center and overlap slightly to make a seam. Bring ends toward center and fold over. Place on greased baking sheet seam side down.

Bake 15 minutes or until filling is heated thoroughly. Crepe will be a pale brown color. Makes 6 filled crepes.

Filling:

Cook snow peas, bean sprouts, and mushrooms in a microwave-safe bowl on HIGH until crisp-tender. In a large bowl, stir together shrimp, cooked vegetables, celery, bell pepper, soy sauce, and salt.

New England Meat Pockets

A wonderful portable meal.

3 cups all-purpose flour
1 teaspoon salt
1 cup solid vegetable shortening
1/2 cup ice water
Meat & Vegetable Filling (see below)
1 egg beaten with 1 tablespoon milk for egg wash

Meat & Vegetable Filling:

1 pound boneless beef stew meat (1/2-inch chunks)
1 tablespoon unseasoned meat tenderizer
3 small carrots, thinly sliced
1 large potato, cut into 1/4-inch squares
1 medium-size onion, minced
1/4 teaspoon pepper
1 (7/8-oz.) package brown gravy mix

Preheat oven to 350°F (175°C). Grease a large baking sheet. In a large bowl, stir together flour and salt. Using a pastry blender, cut in shortening until mixture resembles coarse cornmeal. Stir in just enough ice water to hold dough together. Turn out dough onto a lightly floured board. Knead lightly, then form into a roll and cut into 5 equal pieces. Roll out each dough piece into a circle about 6 inches in diameter.

Prepare filling. Divide filling and spoon (about 1 heaping cup) into center of each dough round. Moisten edges of dough with some of the egg wash. Gently fold dough over to cover filling. Pinch edges tightly together. Using a pastry brush, paint tops with egg wash.

Bake 60 minutes or until golden brown. Serve hot. Makes 5 meat pockets.

Meat & Vegetable Filling:

Sprinkle beef with meat tenderizer according to container directions. In a large bowl, stir together meat, carrots, potato, onion, and pepper. Sprinkle with gravy mix and toss to coat meat and vegetables.

Phyllo-wrapped Brie

Quick, easy, and so delicious! Make the full recipe for a
party or bake only one Brie round for a smaller group.

1 pound phyllo pastry dough
1/4 cup margarine, melted
4 (8-oz.) Brie cheese rounds
Finely chopped parsley

Preheat oven to 400°F (205°C). Grease a large baking sheet. Using a pastry brush and working rapidly, paint every third sheet of phyllo dough with melted margarine, then make a stack of 12 sheets. Cover portion of phyllo that is not being used with plastic wrap or a damp cloth.

Carefully wrap phyllo stack around 1 Brie cheese and place seam side down on baking sheet. Repeat with remaining phyllo, margarine, and cheeses. Paint tops and sides with melted margarine. Sprinkle tops with parsley.

Bake 15 to 20 minutes or until golden brown. Allow to cool 5 minutes before serving. Makes 4 rounds or about 30 appetizers.

Edible Soup Bowls

Another all-in-one meal.
Fill the hollowed out loaf with your favorite hot soup, chowder, or stew.
Eat the soup and the bowl, too.

2 egg whites
1 cup hot water
1 tablespoon sugar
1 teaspoon salt
2 tablespoons margarine, melted
1 (1/4-oz.) package active dry yeast
4 cups whole-wheat flour

In a small bowl, using electric mixer, beat egg whites until very stiff. Set aside. In a large bowl, on low speed, beat together hot water, sugar, salt, and margarine. Sprinkle in yeast and blend well. Add flour gradually, beating after each addition. Remove bowl from mixer and use a spatula to fold in egg whites.

Turn out dough onto a lightly floured board and knead 5 minutes or until smooth. Cover and let rise in a warm place 2 hours or until double in size. Punch dough down, then knead lightly. Divide into 3 round balls. Grease a large baking sheet and space dough balls evenly on sheet. Cover with cloth and let rise 1 hour.

When ready to bake, preheat oven to 350°F (175°C) 10 minutes and place a pan of water on the bottom rack.

Bake loaves on top rack 35 to 40 minutes or until golden brown. When ready to serve, slice off the top of each loaf with a serrated knife and scoop out half of the inside to form a bowl. Fill with your favorite hot soup, chowder, or stew and replace top. Remind your guests that this unique bowl is edible after the soup is gone. Makes 3 edible soup bowls.

Variation

For a French bread–type bowl, substitute white flour.

Mexican Pizza Puffins

This recipe breaks all the rules for muffins, so we call them puffins.

4 cups all-purpose flour
1 teaspoon salt
1 tablespoon sugar
1 (1/4-oz.) package active dry yeast
1 cup warm milk
2 tablespoons margarine, melted and cooled
Spicy Filling (see below)
4 ounces corn chips, broken
1/3 cup sliced ripe olives

Spicy Filling:
1 pound lean ground beef
1 (1-1/8-oz.) package taco seasoning mix
1/4 cup salsa
4-1/2 cups shredded Cheddar cheese (1-1/4 pounds)
1/2 cup chopped onion
1/4 cup chopped green bell pepper

In a large bowl, using electric mixer at low speed, mix together flour, salt, sugar, and yeast. In a small bowl, beat together milk and margarine with a whisk. With mixer on medium speed, gradually beat milk mixture into flour mixture. Knead 5 minutes on a lightly floured board. Cover and let rise in a warm place 1 hour or until double in size.

Prepare filling. Grease a large baking sheet.

Divide dough into 4 balls and flatten each into a circle 6 inches in diameter. Place rounds on baking sheet. Spread 1 tablespoon salsa on each. Divide beef mixture into 4 parts and spoon into center of each dough round. Sprinkle 3-1/2 cups cheese over meat. Top with onion and bell pepper. Bring dough over filling to make a seam and pinch together. Sprinkle with remaining cheese, corn chips, and olives. Let rise in a warm place 1 hour (puffins will spread). Preheat oven to 350F (175°C) 10 minutes.

Bake 20 to 25 minutes or until golden brown. Serve hot. Makes 4 large pizza puffins.

Spicy Filling:

In a medium-size skillet, cook ground beef over medium heat until browned, stirring to break up meat. Stir in taco seasoning mix. Reserve remaining filling ingredients until needed.

Breast o' Chicken Wrap

The filling is similar to a chicken potpie, but you don't need a fork to eat these.

Chicken & Vegetable Filling (see below)
2 cups all-purpose flour
2-1/2 teaspoons baking powder
1/2 cup margarine, chilled
2/3 cup milk
1 egg beaten with 1 tablespoon water for egg wash

Chicken & Vegetable Filling:

2 tablespoons vegetable oil
2/3 cup chopped yellow onion
2/3 cup chopped green onions
1/2 cup chopped green bell pepper
1 cup chopped fresh mushrooms
3 tablespoons cornstarch
1-1/2 cups milk
3 cups cooked and cubed chicken breast
1/2 teaspoon seasoned salt

Preheat oven to 425°F (220°C). Grease a large baking sheet. Prepare filling and refrigerate.

In a large bowl, stir together flour and baking powder. Using a pastry blender, cut in margarine until mixture resembles cornmeal. Stir in milk with a fork. Knead 2 minutes on a lightly floured board. Let dough rest 10 minutes.

Form dough into 6 equal balls. Roll out dough balls into circles 6 inches in diameter.

Divide filling into 6 equal parts (about 2/3 cup each) and place on one-half of each dough circle. Bring edges over to meet and seal by pressing with a fork. Paint tops with egg wash.

Bake 15 minutes or until golden brown. Serve hot. Makes 6 pastries.

Chicken Vegetable Filling:

In a large nonstick skillet, heat oil. Add onion, green onions, bell pepper, and mushrooms and cook 5 minutes over medium heat. Gradually stir in cornstarch. Gradually add milk, stirring constantly. When sauce begins to boil, add chicken and seasoned salt.

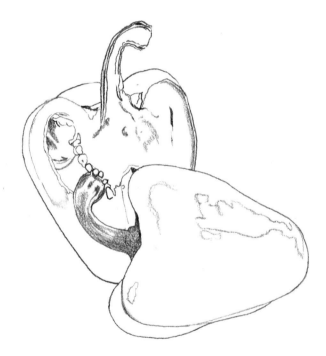

Broccoli & Cheese Yeast Pockets

Eat yeast pockets out of hand, just like a muffin.
Freeze for quick meals.

4 cups all-purpose flour
2 (1/4-oz.) packages active dry yeast
1/3 cup nonfat dried milk powder
1/4 cup sugar
2 teaspoon salt
1/4 cup margarine, melted and cooled
1 egg
1-1/3 cups lukewarm water
5 cups frozen chopped broccoli,
      thawed and cut into very small pieces
6 cups shredded Cheddar cheese (1-1/2 pounds)
2 eggs beaten with 1/2 cup water for egg wash

In a large bowl, stir together flour, yeast, dried milk, sugar, and 1/2 teaspoon of the salt. Set aside. In a medium-size bowl, beat together margarine and 1 egg with a whisk, then beat in water. Using an electric mixer on low speed, gradually add egg mixture to flour mixture and blend well. With mixer on high speed, beat 1 minute. Cover dough and let rise in a warm place 45 minutes or until double in size. When ready, knead dough on lightly floured board 2 minutes. Flour hands, then roll dough into 10 balls. Allow to rest 15 minutes.

Preheat oven to 325°F (165°C). Grease a large baking sheet. Roll out dough balls into circles 3-1/2 to 4 inches in diameter, then brush edges with lukewarm water.

Place broccoli in a medium-size bowl and sprinkle with remaining 1-1/2 teaspoons salt. In center of each dough circle spread 1/2 cup cheese, then 1/2 cup broccoli and top with 1 tablespoon shredded cheese. Bring ends together to enclose filling and pinch edges. Place pockets on baking sheet seam side down. Using a pastry brush, paint tops and sides of yeast pockets with egg wash.

Bake 45 minutes or until golden brown. Serve hot. Makes 10 pastries.

Reduced-Calorie Muffins

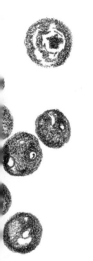

We know some of you want a muffin, even if only occasionally, that is lower in fat and calories. So we went back to the kitchen to create a few wonderful, wiser-choice muffin combinations that you can eat without guilt. We are proud of the delicious results. Jack Sprat would love our muffins!

Low-fat Chocolate Muffins

Guilt-free for dieters—almost no fat.

2 cups all-purpose flour
3 tablespoons cornstarch
1-1/4 cups sugar
1/4 cup unsweetened cocoa powder
1/2 teaspoon salt
2 teaspoons baking soda
1-1/2 cups water
2 teaspoons vinegar
2 teaspoons vanilla extract

Preheat oven to 425°F (220°C). Line 15 (2-3/4-inch) muffin cups with paper liners. In a large bowl, stir together flour, cornstarch, sugar, cocoa, salt, and baking soda.

Stir in water, vinegar, and vanilla. Blend well. (Batter will be thin and somewhat watery.) Fill muffin cups three-quarters full.

Bake 20 minutes or until muffins spring back when lightly touched. Allow to cool in pan 5 minutes. Makes 15 (2-3/4-inch) muffins.

Apple Oat Bran Muffins

A healthy high-fiber muffin with no shortening—very soft and moist.

1 egg
1/2 cup plus 1 tablespoon honey
1/3 cup buttermilk
1/4 cup water
1 cup whole-wheat flour
1/2 cup unprocessed wheat bran
1/2 cup unprocessed oat bran
1/2 teaspoon baking soda
1/2 teaspoon baking powder
1/2 teaspoon ground cinnamon
1 cup coarsely chopped peeled apple
1/2 cup coarsely chopped walnuts or pecans (optional)

Preheat oven to 350°F (175°C). Grease 12 (2-3/4-inch) muffin cups. In a medium-size bowl, beat together egg and honey with a whisk. Beat in buttermilk and water.

In a large bowl, stir together flour, wheat bran, oat bran, baking soda, baking powder, and cinnamon. Add buttermilk mixture, apples, and nuts, if using, to flour mixture and stir just to moisten dry ingredients. Fill muffin cups two-thirds full.

Bake 15 to 20 minutes or until muffins spring back when lightly pressed. Allow to cool in pan 5 minutes. Makes 12 (2-3/4-inch) muffins.

Jack Sprat's Bran Muffins

Finally, a truly good low-cal bran muffin with almost no fat.

1/2 cup golden raisins
3/4 cup hot water
2 cups unprocessed wheat bran
1 cup whole-wheat flour
2 teaspoons baking powder
1/2 teaspoon baking soda
1/2 teaspoon ground cinnamon
1/3 cup packed light brown sugar
2 egg whites
1-1/4 cups skim milk
1 cup applesauce

Preheat oven to 400°F (205°C). Line 14 (2-3/4-inch) muffin cups with paper liners. In a small bowl, stir together raisins and hot water. Set aside.

In a large bowl, stir together bran, flour, baking powder, baking soda, cinnamon, and brown sugar. In a medium-size bowl, lightly beat together egg whites, milk, and applesauce with a whisk. Stir milk mixture into flour mixture. Blend well. Drain and fold in raisins. Fill muffin cups two-thirds full.

Bake 20 minutes or until light brown. Allow to cool in pan 5 minutes. Makes 14 (2-3/4-inch) muffins.

Lite 'n' Healthy Blueberry Muffins

You won't miss the fat.

2 cups all-purpose flour
1-1/3 cups granulated sugar
2/3 cup cornstarch
1 tablespoon baking powder
1 teaspoon salt
1/2 cup nonfat dried milk powder
2-1/2 cups fresh or frozen blueberries
4 egg whites
1 cup water
1 teaspoon vanilla extract
1/2 cup packed light brown sugar

Preheat oven to 400°F (205°C). Line 18 (2-3/4-inch) muffin cups with paper liners. In a large bowl, stir together flour, sugar, cornstarch, baking powder, salt, and dried milk. Stir in blueberries.

In a medium-size bowl, lightly beat together egg whites, water, and vanilla with a whisk. Add egg white mixture to flour mixture and stir just enough to moisten dry ingredients. Fill muffin cups to top and sprinkle with brown sugar.

Bake 30 minutes or until golden brown. Allow to cool in pan 5 minutes. Makes 18 (2-3/4-inch) muffins.

Dinner Muffins

Do you remember when there seemed to be only blueberry and bran muffins? Not anymore. These recipes represent a tremendous variety of colors, textures, flavors, and aromas to perk up any meal and help banish your daily bread routine.

Just lay one or two of these wholesome muffins on a plate, then stand aside and watch the smiles come out as kids and adults alike raid the honey or jam jar and butter dish. These muffins are fine partners for hot soups and crisp salads, too.

One Georgia friend says that it's like "uptown down South" when she serves a basketful of these warm muffin masterpieces for afternoon tea.

Peppery Mozzarella Muffins

A wonderful muffin for brunch when served with jalapeño jelly.

2 cups all-purpose flour
1 tablespoon sugar
1 tablespoon baking powder
1 teaspoon coarsely ground pepper
1/2 teaspoon salt
1/3 cup nonfat dried milk powder
1 egg, well beaten
1/4 cup olive oil
1 cup water
1-1/2 cups shredded mozzarella cheese (6 ounces)

Preheat oven to 400°F (205°C). Heavily grease 12 (2-3/4-inch) muffin cups. In a large bowl, stir together flour, sugar, baking powder, pepper, salt, and dried milk.

In a small bowl, beat together egg, olive oil, and water with a whisk. Pour egg mixture over flour mixture and mix just to moisten dry ingredients. Fold in 1 cup of the cheese.

Fill muffin cups half full and top with remaining cheese.

Bake 15 to 20 minutes or until golden brown. Allow to cool in pan 5 minutes. Makes 12 (2-3/4-inch) muffins.

Hush Puppy Muffins

The terrific taste of Southern hush puppies without the fat.

1-1/2 cups cornmeal
1/2 cup all-purpose flour
3/4 teaspoon baking soda
1/3 teaspoon salt
1/2 cup finely chopped onion
2 eggs, well beaten
1/3 cup vegetable oil
3/4 cup buttermilk

Preheat oven to 450°F (220°C). Grease 12 (2-3/4-inch) muffin cups. In a large bowl, stir together cornmeal, flour, baking soda, and salt. Stir in onion.

In a small bowl, beat together eggs and vegetable oil with a whisk, then beat in buttermilk. Add egg mixture to flour mixture and mix just to moisten dry ingredients. Fill muffin cups two-thirds full.

Bake 20 minutes or until brown and crusty on top. Makes 12 (2-3/4-inch) muffins. Allow to cool in pan 5 minutes.

Full-of-Fiber Wheat Bran Muffins

Have your daily fiber in a muffin.

3/4 cup golden raisins
1 cup hot water
2-1/2 cups unprocessed wheat bran
1-1/2 cups whole-wheat flour
1/2 cup packed light brown sugar
1 teaspoon baking powder
1/2 teaspoon salt
1/2 teaspoon baking soda
2 eggs, well beaten
1/2 cup vegetable oil
1 cup buttermilk
1 cup water

Preheat oven to 375°F (190°C). Line 12 (2-3/4-inch) muffin cups with paper liners. In a small bowl, cover raisins with hot water. Set aside.

In a large bowl, stir together wheat bran, whole-wheat flour, brown sugar, baking powder, salt, and baking soda. In a medium-size bowl, beat together eggs, vegetable oil, buttermilk, and water with a whisk. Add egg mixture to bran mixture and mix just to moisten dry ingredients. Drain and fold in raisins. Fill muffin cups three-quarters full.

Bake 20 minutes or until golden brown. Allow to cool in pan 5 minutes. Makes 12 (2-3/4-inch) muffins.

Variation

Muffin Tops: Refrigerate batter for 1 hour to firm. Preheat oven to 450°F (230°C). Spray 2 baking sheets with nonstick cooking spray. Drop batter on baking sheets with a 1/4-cup measure or scoop. Bake 25 minutes or until golden brown. Remove and cool on wire racks. Makes 15 tops.

Veggie Corn Muffins

A wonderful complement for soups or chili.

1 cup all-purpose flour
1/2 cup cornmeal
1 tablespoon sugar
1 tablespoon baking powder
1/2 teaspoon salt
1 teaspoon Italian seasoning
1/8 teaspoon dried minced garlic
2 eggs, well beaten
1 tablespoon olive oil
1/2 cup skim milk
1/2 cup canned or cooked whole-kernel corn, drained
1/2 cup finely chopped green bell pepper
1/4 cup finely chopped onion

Preheat oven to 400°F (205°C). Line 12 (2-3/4-inch) muffin cups with paper liners. In a large bowl, stir together flour, cornmeal, sugar, baking powder, salt, Italian seasoning, and garlic.

In a medium-size bowl, beat together eggs, olive oil, and milk with a whisk, then stir in corn, bell pepper, and onion. Pour egg mixture over flour mixture and stir until vegetables are distributed evenly. Fill each muffin cup half full.

Bake 15 to 20 minutes or until golden brown. Allow to cool in pan 5 minutes. Makes 12 (2-3/4-inch) muffins.

Bev's Best Blueberry Muffins

These fragrant favorites are best served warm.

2 eggs
1-1/3 cups milk
1-1/2 cups fresh blueberries
3 cups all-purpose flour
1-1/3 cups sugar
4 teaspoons baking powder
1/2 teaspoon salt
1/2 cup butter-flavored solid vegetable shortening

Preheat oven to 375°F (190°C). Grease 18 (2-3/4-inch) muffin cups. In a small bowl, using an electric mixer at high speed, beat eggs well. Blend in milk at low speed. Coat blueberries with 1/4 cup of the flour.

In a large bowl, stir together remaining flour, sugar, baking powder, and salt. Using a pastry blender, cut in shortening until mixture resembles cornmeal.

Stir in milk mixture just to moisten dry ingredients, then stir in blueberries. Fill muffin cups three-quarters full.

Bake 20 minutes or until golden brown and muffins spring back when lightly touched. Allow to cool in pan 5 minutes. Makes 18 (2-3/4-inch) muffins.

Note

Coating berries in flour keeps them from sinking to the bottom of the muffins.

Two-Week Buttermilk Bran Muffins

*Bake up a batch today, then refrigerate leftover batter in a
covered container for quick breakfasts or snacks.*

2 cups boiling water
2 cups Bran Buds cereal
2 cups sugar
1/2 cup margarine, softened
1/2 cup solid vegetable shortening
4 eggs (preferably pasteurized)
1 quart buttermilk
5 cups all-purpose flour
5 teaspoons baking soda
1 teaspoon salt
4 cups All Bran cereal

Preheat oven to 400°F (205°C). Grease up to 36 (2-3/4-inch) muffin cups. In a medium-size bowl, stir together boiling water and Bran Buds cereal. Set aside to cool.

In a large bowl, using an electric mixer at high speed, beat together sugar, margarine, and vegetable shortening. Add eggs, one at a time, beating well after each. Stir in buttermilk, then cereal mixture. In an extra-large bowl, stir together flour, baking soda, and salt. Stir in All Bran cereal.

Add buttermilk mixture to flour mixture all at once and stir to moisten. Fill muffin cups two-thirds full and bake 15 to 20 minutes or until muffins spring back when lightly pressed. Allow to cool in pan 5 minutes.

Refrigerate leftover batter in a covered container up to 2 weeks. For variety, add nuts, raisins, or other fruits before baking. Makes 36 (2-3/4-inch) muffins.

Honey Wheat Yeast Muffins

The flavor of this unique and delicious muffin is enhanced by yeast.

1 cup vegetable oil
3/4 cup honey
1 cup hot water
1 teaspoon salt
2 (1/4-oz.) packages active dry yeast
1 cup lukewarm water
2 eggs, slightly beaten
6 cups whole-wheat flour

Preheat oven to 350°F (175°C). Grease 30 (2-3/4-inch) muffin cups. In the large bowl of an electric mixer, using the dough paddle, blend together vegetable oil, honey, hot water, and salt. Beat in yeast and lukewarm water, stirring until yeast dissolves (about 7 minutes). Continue using dough paddle to beat in eggs, then gradually beat in flour. Blend well.

Cover bowl and place in refrigerator at least 3 hours (preferably overnight). Stir batter down every hour during the first few hours of refrigeration.

When ready to bake, remove dough from refrigerator and allow to reach room temperature. Using a spatula and spoon (dough will be soft), fill muffin cups two-thirds full. Allow batter to rise to top of cups, about 30 minutes.

Bake 20 minutes or until golden brown. Allow to cool in pan 5 minutes. Makes 30 (2-3/4-inch) muffins.

Broccoli Buttermilk Muffins

This recipe contains a full two cups of vitamin-rich broccoli.
For an even more nutritious muffin use high-lysine cornmeal.

1 cup all-purpose flour
1/2 cup cornmeal
1 tablespoon sugar
1 tablespoon baking powder
1 teaspoon salt
2 teaspoons Italian seasoning
2 cups finely chopped cooked broccoli
2 eggs, well beaten
2 tablespoons olive oil
1 cup buttermilk

Preheat oven to 400°F (205°C). Grease 12 (2-3/4-inch) muffin cups. In a large bowl, stir together flour, cornmeal, sugar, baking powder, salt, and Italian seasoning. Stir in broccoli.

In a small bowl, beat together eggs and olive oil with a whisk, then beat in buttermilk. Add buttermilk mixture to flour mixture and stir just to moisten dry ingredients. Fill muffin cups half full.

Bake 20 minutes or until muffins spring back when lightly touched. Allow to cool in pan 5 minutes. Makes 12 (2-3/4-inch) muffins.

Eat Your Veggies Muffins

Mother was right after all, it is important to eat your vegetables.

1 cup all-purpose flour
1/2 cup cornmeal
4 teaspoons baking powder
2 teaspoons sugar
1 teaspoon salt
1/8 teaspoon red (cayenne) pepper
1/4 cup nonfat dried milk powder
1/4 cup chopped fresh tomato (seeds removed)
1/4 cup finely chopped celery
1/4 cup chopped jalapeño chiles
1/4 cup chopped red bell pepper
1/4 cup chopped green bell pepper
2 eggs, well beaten
1/4 cup olive oil
1/4 cup water

Preheat oven to 400°F (205°C). Grease 12 (2-3/4-inch) muffin cups. In a large bowl stir together flour, cornmeal, baking powder, sugar, salt, cayenne, and dried milk. Stir in tomato, celery, jalapeño chiles, and bell peppers.

In a small bowl, beat together eggs and olive oil with a whisk. Beat in water. Stir into cornmeal mixture just to moisten dry ingredients. Fill muffin cups three-quarters full.

Bake 20 to 25 minutes or until golden brown. Allow to cool in pan 5 minutes. Makes 12 (2-3/4-inch) muffins.

Big Top Blueberry Muffins

This muffin pops over the top while baking—another wonderful variation of everybody's favorite blueberry muffin.

3 cups all-purpose flour
3/4 cup sugar
4 teaspoons baking powder
1/2 teaspoon salt
1/4 cup nonfat dried milk powder
2 cups fresh or frozen blueberries
2 eggs, well beaten
1/2 cup margarine, melted and cooled
1 cup water

Preheat oven to 400°F (205°C). Line 14 (2-3/4-inch) muffin cups with paper liners. In a large bowl, stir together flour, sugar, baking powder, salt, and dried milk. Stir in blueberries.

In a small bowl, beat together eggs, margarine, and water with a whisk. Add egg mixture to flour mixture and stir just to moisten dry ingredients. Fill muffin cups three-quarters full.

Bake 20 minutes or until golden brown. Allow to cool in pan 5 minutes. Makes 14 (2-3/4-inch) muffins.

Variation

Muffin Tops: Refrigerate batter for 1 hour to firm. Preheat oven to 450°F (230°C). Spray 2 baking sheets with nonstick cooking spray. Drop batter on baking sheet with a 1/4-cup measure or scoop. Bake 25 minutes or until browned and tops spring back when touched. Remove and cool on wire racks. Makes 15 tops.

Granola Muffins

Use a good-quality granola for this one.

1-1/2 cups granola cereal
3 cups all-purpose flour
4 teaspoons baking powder
1 cup packed light brown sugar
1/2 teaspoon salt
1/2 cup raisins
2 eggs, well beaten
1/2 cup margarine, melted and cooled
1 cup milk
1/2 teaspoon maple flavoring

Preheat oven to 400°F (205°C). Line 16 (2-3/4-inch) muffin cups with paper liners. Reserve whole nuts from granola for garnishing, if desired. In a large bowl, stir together flour, baking powder, brown sugar, salt, granola, and raisins.

In a small bowl, beat together eggs, margarine, milk, and maple flavoring with a whisk. Add egg mixture to granola mixture and stir just to moisten dry ingredients. Fill muffin cups two-thirds full and garnish with reserved nuts.

Bake 20 minutes or until golden brown. Allow to cool in pan 5 minutes. Makes 16 (2-3/4-inch) muffins.

Banana Oat Bran Muffin

These were a staple in Bev's Puffin' Muffin shops from Day One. Delicious and nutritious.

1/2 cup golden raisins
1/2 cup hot water
1 egg
1 cup packed light brown sugar
1/2 cup vegetable oil
1 teaspoon vanilla extract
2 ripe bananas, mashed (1 cup)
3/4 cup all-purpose flour
3/4 cup whole-wheat flour
2 teaspoons baking powder
1/2 teaspoon baking soda
1/2 cup unprocessed oat bran
1/2 teaspoon ground allspice

Preheat oven to 350°F (175°C). Grease 12 (2-3/4-inch) muffin cups. In a small bowl, cover raisins with hot water. Set aside. In a medium-size bowl, using an electric mixer at medium speed, beat together egg and brown sugar until smooth. Beat in oil and vanilla, blending well. Stir in mashed bananas.

In a large bowl, stir together all-purpose flour, whole-wheat flour, baking powder, and baking soda. Stir in oat bran and allspice. Add banana mixture to flour mixture and stir just to moisten dry ingredients. Drain and fold in raisins. Fill muffin cups two-thirds full.

Bake 20 minutes or until a wooden pick inserted in muffins comes out clean. Allow to cool in pan 5 minutes. Makes 12 (2-3/4-inch) muffins.

Variation

Reduced-fat Banana Muffins: Omit vegetable oil and increase number of bananas to three.

Cheesy Raisin Muffins

Cheese and raisins make these muffins moist.

1 cup golden raisins
1-1/2 cups hot water
2 cups all-purpose flour
4 teaspoons baking powder
1/2 teaspoon salt
1 teaspoon paprika
1/4 cup margarine, chilled
1 egg, well beaten
1 cup evaporated milk
1 cup shredded Cheddar cheese (4 ounces)

Preheat oven to 400°F (205°C). Grease 12 (2-3/4-inch) muffin cups. In a small bowl, cover raisins with hot water. Set aside. In a large bowl, stir together flour, baking powder, salt, and paprika.

Using a pastry blender, cut in margarine until mixture resembles coarse cornmeal. In a medium-size bowl, beat together egg and milk using a whisk. Stir in cheese. Add cheese mixture to flour mixture and stir just to moisten dry ingredients. Drain raisins well and stir into batter. Fill muffin cups two-thirds full.

Bake 20 minutes or until golden brown. Allow to cool in pan 5 minutes. Makes 12 (2-3/4-inch) muffins.

Summer Squash Muffins

An unusual taste that keeps you coming back for more.

2 cups all-purpose flour
1 tablespoon baking powder
2 tablespoons sugar
1/3 teaspoon salt
1 egg, well beaten
2 tablespoons vegetable oil
2/3 cup milk
2/3 cup grated summer squash

Preheat oven to 400°F (205°C). Grease 12 (2-3/4-inch) muffin cups. In a large bowl, stir together flour, baking powder, sugar, and salt. In a medium-size bowl, beat together egg and oil with a whisk, then beat in milk. Stir in squash. Add squash mixture to flour mixture and stir just to moisten dry ingredients. Fill muffin cups half full.

Bake 20 minutes or until muffins spring back when lightly pressed. Allow to cool in pan 5 minutes. Makes 12 (2-3/4-inch) muffins.

Hearty Buckwheat Muffins

Good old-fashioned country fare ready in no time at all.

3/4 cup all-purpose flour
3/4 cup buckwheat flour
2 teaspoons baking powder
3/4 teaspoon salt
1 egg
1 cup water
1/4 cup vegetable oil
1/3 cup honey
3/4 teaspoon vanilla extract
3/4 cup raisins
1/4 cup chopped nuts

Preheat oven to 350°F (175°C). Grease 12 (2-3/4-inch) muffin cups. In a medium-size bowl, stir together all-purpose flour, buckwheat flour, baking powder, and salt.

In a small bowl, beat egg well with a whisk. Beat in water, vegetable oil, honey, and vanilla. Stir egg mixture into flour mixture just until moistened. Lightly stir in raisins and nuts. Batter will appear somewhat thin. Fill muffin cups two-thirds full.

Bake 25 minutes or until edges are lightly browned. Allow to cool in pan 5 minutes. Makes 12 (2-3/4-inch) muffins.

Variation

Stir in 1/3 cup finely chopped apple or dates. Buckwheat lovers can use buckwheat honey.

Yummy Date Muffins

Get your oats here.

1 cup rolled oats
3/4 cup chopped dates
1 cup water
1-1/2 cups all-purpose flour
1/2 cup nonfat dried milk powder
2 teaspoons baking powder
1/2 teaspoon salt
2 large eggs
1/4 cup margarine, melted and cooled
2/3 cup packed light brown sugar
1/2 teaspoon grated lemon zest
1/2 cup chopped pecans

Preheat oven to 400°F (205°C). Line 12 (2-3/4-inch) muffin cups with paper liners. In a large bowl, stir together rolled oats, dates, and water. Set aside.

In a medium-size bowl, stir together flour, dried milk, baking powder, and salt. In a small bowl, beat eggs well with a whisk, then beat in margarine, brown sugar, and lemon zest; stir in pecans. Stir egg mixture into oat mixture and blend well. Fold in flour mixture, stirring just enough to moisten dry ingredients. Fill muffin cups two-thirds full.

Bake 30 minutes or until golden brown. Allow to cool in pan 5 minutes. Makes 12 (2-3/4-inch) muffins.

Zucchini Walnut Muffin

Zucchini are available year round, so make this spicy muffin anytime.

1/2 cup golden raisins
3/4 cup hot water
2 cups all-purpose flour
3/4 cup sugar
3/4 teaspoon baking powder
3/4 teaspoon baking soda
1/2 teaspoon salt
1 teaspoon cinnamon
1/2 teaspoon ground ginger
1/4 teaspoon freshly grated nutmeg
3 eggs, well beaten
1/2 cup vegetable oil
2 teaspoons vanilla extract
1 cup grated zucchini, drained
1/2 cup chopped walnuts

Preheat oven to 375°F (190°C.) Line 18 (2-3/4-inch) muffin cups with paper liners. In a small bowl, cover raisins with hot water. Set aside.

In a large bowl, stir together flour, sugar, baking powder, baking soda, salt, cinnamon, ginger, and nutmeg. In a small bowl, beat together eggs, vegetable oil, and vanilla with a whisk. Stir egg mixture into flour mixture just to moisten dry ingredients. Drain raisins. Stir in zucchini, walnuts, and raisins. Fill muffin cups half full.

Bake 20 minutes or until light brown. Allow to cool in pan 5 minutes. Makes 18 (2-3/4-inch) muffins.

Southern Cracklin' Muffins

A real taste of the South.

1 cup cracklings
1 cup cornmeal
1 cup all-purpose flour
4 teaspoons baking powder
2 teaspoons sugar
1 teaspoon salt
2 eggs
1 cup milk

Preheat oven to 425°F (220°C). Grease 12 (2-3/4-inch) muffin cups. In a small shallow pan, bake cracklings 10 minutes.

While cracklings are baking, in a large bowl stir together cornmeal, flour, baking powder, sugar, and salt. Set aside.

In a small bowl, beat eggs well with a whisk, then beat in milk. Stir egg mixture into cornmeal mixture, then stir in hot cracklings and drippings. Fill muffin cups two-thirds full.

Bake 10 minutes. Turn oven temperature to broil and broil about 1 minute to complete browning muffins without drying them out. Allow to cool in pan 5 minutes. Makes 12 (2-3/4-inch) muffins.

Note

Cracklings are the crunchy pieces of pork fat or skin after rendering out the fat.

Dessert Muffins

Cobbler muffins packed full of plump berries? Koffee Kake Muffins—good with a steaming cup of coffee? Strawberries & Cream Muffins? Why didn't someone think of these before? All are here in this sweet chapter to satisfy anyone with an affection for confections, in what my mom called "ample sufficiency."

Most are quick to make and are lighter and softer in texture than bread-type muffins. They are a welcome treat to top off any meal or to tame your backyard tribe when four o'clock munchies strike. Wrap one in foil, tie with a ribbon, and add to a lunchbox along with a note when life becomes too routine.

Koffee Kake Muffins

Just right for Sunday morning breakfast.

1-1/2 cups all-purpose flour
2 teaspoons baking powder
1/2 cup sugar
1/4 teaspoon salt
1/4 cup margarine, chilled
1 egg, well beaten
1/2 cup milk

Nut Layer/Topping:

1/2 cup packed light brown sugar
2 tablespoons all-purpose flour
2 teaspoons ground cinnamon
1/2 cup chopped walnuts
2 tablespoons margarine, melted

Preheat oven to 375°F (190°C). Line 12 (2-3/4-inch) muffin cups with paper liners. In a large bowl, stir together flour, baking powder, sugar, and salt. Using a pastry blender, cut in margarine until mixture resembles cornmeal.

In a small bowl, beat together egg and milk with a whisk, then add to flour mixture. Stir just to moisten dry ingredients. Prepare topping. Spoon 1 tablespoon batter on bottom of each cup. Add a layer of topping. Repeat layers of batter and topping until cups are three-quarters full, ending with topping.

Bake 20 minutes or until muffins spring back when lightly pressed. Allow to cool in pan 5 minutes. Makes 12 (2-3/4-inch) muffins.

Nut Layer Topping:

In a small bowl, stir together sugar, flour, cinnamon, and walnuts. Stir in melted margarine.

Buckwheat Apple Muffins

A healthy way to get grains and fruit into your diet.

5 cups coarsely chopped peeled apples
1 cup sugar
3 eggs, lightly beaten
1/2 cup vegetable oil
2 teaspoons vanilla extract
1 cup buckwheat flour
1 cup whole-wheat flour
2 teaspoons baking soda
1-1/2 teaspoons ground cinnamon
1 teaspoon salt
1-1/4 cups raisins
1-1/2 cups coarsely chopped walnuts

Preheat oven to 325°F (165°C). Grease 18 (2-3/4-inch) muffin cups. In a large bowl, stir together apples and sugar.

In a small bowl, beat together eggs, vegetable oil, and vanilla with a whisk, then stir into the apple mixture. In a medium-size bowl, stir together buckwheat flour, whole-wheat flour, baking soda, cinnamon, and salt. Fold flour mixture into apple mixture, stirring just enough to moisten dry ingredients. Stir in raisins and walnuts. Batter will be lumpy with fruits and nuts. Fill muffin cups three-quarters full.

Bake 25 to 30 minutes, or until very firm to the touch and medium-brown in appearance. Allow to cool in pan 5 minutes. Makes 18 (2-3/4-inch) muffins.

Coconut Pecan Muffins

This generous recipe makes forty marvelous muffins. Leftovers are truly better the second day. Tightly wrap cooled muffins and freeze them for up to two months.

1 cup margarine, softened
1-1/2 cups sugar
4 eggs
4-1/2 cups all-purpose flour
1 tablespoon baking powder
1 teaspoon baking soda
1/2 teaspoon salt
1 (15-oz.) can cream of coconut
1 cup sour cream
2 cups flaked sweetened coconut (about 6 ounces)
1 cup coarsely chopped pecans

Preheat oven to 325°F (165°C). Grease 40 (2-3/4-inch) muffin cups. In a large bowl, using an electric mixer on high speed, beat together margarine and sugar. Beat in eggs, one at a time, beating thoroughly after each one.

In a medium-size bowl, stir together flour, baking powder, baking soda, and salt. Fold cream of coconut and sour cream into margarine mixture alternately with flour mixture, beginning and ending with flour. Lightly stir in coconut and pecans. Fill muffin cups two-thirds full.

Bake 20 minutes or until golden brown and muffins spring back when lightly touched. Allow to cool in pan 5 minutes. Makes 40 (2-3/4-inch) muffins.

Blackberry Cobbler Muffins

Bake up the best of summer's berry bounty without all the effort of shortcake or pie.
Easy to reheat in the microwave.

2 cups blackberries, fresh or frozen
2-1/3 cups sugar
2 eggs
1/2 cup butter-flavored solid vegetable shortening, melted
1 cup milk
3 cups all-purpose flour
1/2 teaspoon salt
4 teaspoons baking powder

Preheat oven to 325°F (165°C). Grease 18 (2-3/4-inch) muffin cups. In a small bowl, stir together berries and 1 cup of the sugar. Set aside.

In a medium-size bowl, using an electric mixer at medium speed, beat together eggs and shortening. Beat in milk at low speed. In a large bowl, stir together flour, remaining 1-1/3 cups sugar, salt, and baking powder. Add milk mixture to flour mixture and stir just to moisten dry ingredients. Gently stir in berries. Fill muffin cups three-quarters full.

Bake 20 minutes or until golden brown and muffins spring back when lightly touched. Allow to cool in pan 10 minutes before serving. Makes 18 (2-3/4-inch) muffins.

Tangy Lemon Pudding Muffins

An elegant sweet muffin baked in giant cups.
Turn each upside down and top with a cheery half-cherry.

1 cup sugar
1/4 cup all-purpose flour
1/8 teaspoon salt
3 tablespoons butter, melted and cooled
2 teaspoons grated lemon zest
1/4 cup fresh lemon juice
1-1/2 cups milk
3 eggs, separated
2 maraschino cherries, halved

Preheat oven to 325°F (165°C). Grease 4 giant muffin cups. In a large bowl, stir together sugar, flour, and salt. Stir in melted butter, lemon zest, and lemon juice.

In a small bowl, beat together milk and egg yolks with a whisk. Stir milk mixture into flour mixture. Blend well. In a medium-size bowl, using an electric mixer, beat egg whites until very stiff. Fold egg whites gently into batter. Fill muffin cups to the top.

Bake 45 minutes or until muffins spring back when lightly touched and are golden brown. Allow muffins to cool in pan, then turn out on a baking sheet. Place each upside down in a giant paper muffin cup liner and top with a half cherry. Makes 4 giant muffins.

Marzipan Muffins

A rich, moist, and tender muffin with a sugary almond-laden top.

1/2 cup margarine, softened
8 ounces almond paste
1-1/2 cups sugar plus extra for sprinkling
3 eggs
2 cups all-purpose flour
1 teaspoon baking powder
1/8 teaspoon salt
1 cup milk
1/3 cup slivered blanched almonds

Preheat oven to 350°F (175°C). Grease 12 (2-3/4-inch) muffin cups. In a large bowl, using an electric mixer at high speed, beat together margarine and almond paste. Gradually add 1-1/2 cups sugar and eggs, beating well after each addition.

In a small bowl, stir together flour, baking powder, and salt. Alternately add the milk and flour mixture to the margarine mixture, ending with flour and stirring just enough to moisten dry ingredients. Fill muffin cups three-quarters full. Sprinkle tops with almonds, then sugar.

Bake 18 minutes or until muffins spring back when lightly touched. Allow to cool in pan 5 minutes. Makes 12 (2-3/4-inch) muffins.

Note

Watch these muffins with extra care while baking and remove from the oven at just the right time so almonds do not burn.

Strawberries & Cream Muffins

Mouthwatering—just right for strawberry season.

1/2 cup margarine, softened
1 cup sugar
1/2 teaspoon vanilla extract
1/4 teaspoon lemon extract
2 eggs
2 cups all-purpose flour
1/2 teaspoon salt
1/2 teaspoon baking soda
1/2 cup sour cream
2 cups sliced strawberries

Preheat oven to 350°F (175°C). Line 18 (2-3/4-inch) muffin cups with paper liners. In a large bowl, using electric mixer on medium speed, beat together margarine, sugar, vanilla, and lemon extract until light and fluffy. Beat in eggs, one at a time, beating well after each.

In a small bowl, stir together flour, salt, and baking soda. On low speed, fold flour mixture into sugar mixture alternately with sour cream. Add strawberries and beat on low 2 minutes to break up berries. Fill muffin cups two-thirds full.

Bake 25 minutes or until muffins spring back when lightly touched. Allow to cool in pan 10 minutes. Makes 18 (2-3/4-inch) muffins.

Eden's Delight Muffin

A cakelike muffin with Garden of Eden lusciousness.

1-1/4 cups sugar
2 eggs
1/4 cup vegetable oil
1/2 teaspoon vanilla extract
2 cups all-purpose flour
1/2 teaspoon baking powder
1/2 teaspoon baking soda
1/4 teaspoon salt
1/2 teaspoon ground cinnamon
3 large Granny Smith apples, finely chopped (about 2-1/2 cups)
1 cup chopped nuts

Preheat oven to 400°F (205°C). Line 12 (2-3/4-inch) muffin cups with paper liners. In a large bowl, beat together sugar and eggs with electric mixer until well blended. Beat in oil and vanilla. Set aside.

In another large bowl, stir together flour, baking powder, baking soda, salt, and cinnamon. Stir in apples and nuts. Stir apple mixture into egg mixture. Beat 5 minutes on medium speed. Fill muffin cups three-fourths full.

Bake 20 minutes or until golden brown. Allow to cool in pan 5 minutes. Makes 12 (2-3/4-inch) muffins.

Note

This muffin, unlike most, requires extra beating to release apple juices needed for moistness.

Nut 'n' Muffins

This nutty treat has a light texture and a crunchy peanut topping.

1/2 cup peanut butter
1/3 cup margarine, softened
1 teaspoon vanilla extract
1-1/2 cups packed light brown sugar
2 eggs
2 cups all-purpose flour
2 teaspoons baking powder
1/4 teaspoon salt
3/4 cup milk
1 cup coarsely chopped unsalted peanuts

Peanut Topping:

1-1/2 cups peanut butter
3/4 cup powdered sugar
1/2 cup finely chopped unsalted peanuts

Preheat oven to 350°F (175°C). Grease 18 (2-3/4-inch) muffin cups. In a large bowl using electric mixer at high speed, beat together peanut butter, margarine, and vanilla. Gradually add brown sugar, then eggs, beating well after each.

In a medium-size bowl, stir together flour, baking powder, and salt. Fold flour mixture alternately with milk into peanut butter mixture, stirring just to moisten. Stir in peanuts. Fill muffin cups half full.

Bake 20 minutes or until muffins spring back when lightly touched. Prepare topping and spread on warm muffins. Makes 18 (2-3/4-inch) muffins.

Peanut Topping:

Using electric mixer at medium speed, beat together peanut butter and sugar. Spread on warm muffins. Sprinkle with finely chopped peanuts.

Tropical Fruit Muffins

Serve these fruity muffins instead of coffeecake or doughnuts.

2 cups all-purpose flour
1-1/3 cups sugar
1 teaspoon baking soda
1/2 teaspoon salt
1 (15-1/2-oz.) can fruit cocktail
2 eggs, well beaten
1/2 teaspoon vanilla extract
1 cup coarsely chopped pecans
2/3 cup packed light brown sugar, tightly packed
Coconut Topping (see below)
12 maraschino cherries, halved

Coconut Topping:

1 cup margarine
1 (14-oz.) can condensed milk
1 (14-oz.) package flaked sweetened coconut

Preheat oven to 325°F (165°C). Grease 24 (2-3/4-inch) muffin cups. In a large bowl, stir together flour, sugar, baking soda, and salt. Stir in fruit cocktail with juice, eggs, and vanilla. Blend well. Fill muffin cups just half full. Set aside.

In a small bowl, stir together pecans and brown sugar. Sprinkle over batter. Bake 20 minutes or until golden brown and springy to the touch. Prepare topping and spoon over hot muffins in cups. Top each muffin with a maraschino cherry half. Allow to cool in pan 5 minutes. Makes 24 (2-3/4-inch) muffins.

Coconut Topping:

While muffins are baking, melt margarine in a large microwave-safe bowl on HIGH. Cool. Stir in condensed milk and coconut.

Banana Nut Muffins

A real old-fashioned taste.

1 cup packed light brown sugar
1/2 cup margarine, softened
2 eggs
3 ripe bananas
2 cups all-purpose flour
1 teaspoon baking soda
1/4 cup buttermilk
1 cup chopped nuts

Preheat oven to 400°F (205°C). Line 14 (2-3/4-inch) muffin cups with paper liners. In a large bowl, using electric mixer at medium speed, beat together brown sugar and margarine until light and fluffy. Add eggs, one at a time, beating well after each. In a medium-size bowl, mash bananas and beat into sugar mixture.

In another medium-size bowl, stir together flour and baking soda. At low speed, alternately beat in flour mixture and buttermilk to banana mixture, starting and ending with flour. Stir in chopped nuts. Fill muffin cups two-thirds full.

Bake 20 minutes or until golden brown and muffins spring back when lightly touched. Allow to cool in pan 5 minutes. Makes 14 (2-3/4-inch) muffins.

Tutti Fruity Mini-Muffins

Blueberries, bananas, and yogurt. A delicious combination.

1 egg
1/4 cup vegetable oil
1/2 cup sugar
1/2 cup (1 medium-size) mashed banana
1/4 cup plain yogurt
1/2 teaspoon vanilla extract
1 cup all-purpose flour
1/2 teaspoon baking soda
1/4 teaspoon salt
2/3 cup frozen blueberries, unthawed

Preheat oven to 350°F (175°C). Spray 24 mini-muffin cups. In a large bowl, beat together egg and oil with a whisk. Beat in sugar. Stir in mashed banana, yogurt, and vanilla.

In a medium-size bowl, stir together flour, baking soda, and salt, then gently stir in frozen blueberries. Gently stir flour mixture into banana mixture just to moisten dry ingredients. Fill muffin cups two-thirds full.

Bake 15 to 18 minutes or until golden brown. Allow to cool in pan 5 minutes. Makes 24 mini-muffins.

Lemon Muffin Cakes

Perfect to serve with your favorite hot or cold tea.

1 cup margarine, softened
1 cup sugar
4 eggs
2 teaspoons lemon extract
1-3/4 cups all-purpose flour
1/2 teaspoon baking powder
1/2 teaspoon salt

Preheat oven to 350°F (175°C). Line 12 (2-3/4-inch) muffin cups with paper liners. In a large bowl, beat together margarine and sugar until light and frothy, using an electric mixer. Beat in eggs, one at a time, beating after each. Beat in lemon extract.

In a medium-size bowl, stir together flour, baking powder, and salt. Gradually add flour mixture to margarine mixture with mixer on lowest speed, occasionally scraping down sides of bowl with spatula. Fill muffin cups two-thirds full.

Bake 20 minutes or until golden brown and muffins spring back when lightly touched. Allow to cool in pan 5 minutes. Makes 12 cupcake muffins.

Mother's Yellow Lemon Cups

Light, delicate, and elegant! Perfect to serve to friends on special occasions.

1/2 cup margarine, softened
1/4 cup solid vegetable shortening
1-1/2 cups sugar
3 eggs
1/2 teaspoon vanilla extract
1/2 teaspoon lemon extract
1-1/2 cups all-purpose flour
1/2 teaspoon baking powder
1/2 cup milk

Preheat oven to 400°F (205°C). Grease 16 (2-3/4-inch) muffin cups. In a large bowl, with electric mixer at high speed, beat together margarine, vegetable shortening, and sugar until light and fluffy. Beat in eggs, one at a time, beating after each. Beat in vanilla and lemon extracts.

In a medium-size bowl, stir together flour and baking powder. With mixer on low, add flour mixture to margarine mixture alternately with milk, beginning and ending with flour. Blend well. Fill muffin cups two-thirds full.

Bake 20 minutes or until tops begin to brown. Allow to cool in pan 5 minutes. Makes 16 (2-3/4-inch) muffins.

Chocolate Brownie Muffins

This muffin has a crusty cookielike top with a yummy moist center. No leavening agents are needed.

4 ounces (4 squares) semisweet chocolate
1/2 ounce (1/2 square) unsweetened chocolate
1 cup margarine
1 cup all-purpose flour
1-1/2 cups sugar
1-1/2 cups coarsely chopped pecans
4 eggs, well beaten

Preheat oven to 325°F (165°C). Heavily grease 14 (2-3/4-inch) muffin cups. Melt chocolate squares and margarine together in a medium-size double boiler or in a microwave-safe bowl in a microwave. Set aside to cool.

In a large bowl, stir together flour, sugar, and pecans. Stir in eggs thoroughly, then the cooled chocolate mixture. Blend well. Fill muffin cups to the top.

Bake about 40 minutes or until a wooden pick inserted in muffins comes out clean. Allow to cool in pan 5 minutes. Makes 14 (2-3/4-inch) muffins.

Note

Do not use paper cup liners for these muffins, because they may be difficult to remove.

Metric Conversion Charts

Comparison to Metric Measure				
When You Know	**Symbol**	**Multiply By**	**To Find**	**Symbol**
teaspoons	tsp	5.0	milliliters	ml
tablespoons	tbsp	15.0	milliliters	ml
fluid ounces	fl. oz.	30.0	milliliters	ml
cups	c.	0.24	liters	l
pints	pt.	0.47	liters	l
quarts	qt.	0.95	liters	l
ounces	oz.	28.0	grams	g
pounds	lb.	0.45	kilograms	kg
Fahrenheit	F	5/9 (after subtracting 32)	Celsius	C

Liquid Measure to Milliliters

1/4 teaspoon	=	1.25 milliliters
1/2 teaspoon	=	2.5 milliliters
3/4 teaspoon	=	3.75 milliliters
1 teaspoon	=	5.0 milliliters
1-1/4 teaspoons	=	6.25 milliliters
1-1/2 teaspoons	=	7.5 milliliters
1-3/4 teaspoons	=	8.75 milliliters
2 teaspoons	=	10.0 milliliters
1 tablespoon	=	15.0 milliliters
2 tablespoons	=	30.0 milliliters

Fahrenheit to Celsius

F	C
200-205	95
220-225	105
245-250	120
275	135
300-305	150
325-330	165
345-350	175
370-375	190
400-405	205
425-430	220
445-450	230
470-475	245
500	260

Liquid Measure to Liters

1/4 cup	=	0.06 liters
1/2 cup	=	0.12 liters
3/4 cup	=	0.18 liters
1 cup	=	0.24 liters
1-1/4 cups	=	0.3 liters
1-1/2 cups	=	0.36 liters
2 cups	=	0.48 liters
2-1/2 cups	=	0.6 liters
3 cups	=	0.72 liters
3-1/2 cups	=	0.84 liters
4 cups	=	0.96 liters
4-1/2 cups	=	1.08 liters
5 cups	=	1.2 liters
5-1/2 cups	=	1.32 liters

Index

Beverly Walker Worrell

Being an author is a first for Beverly Worrell—but she is already thinking of another project. There aren't many things that she hasn't tried in her 20 years as an entrepreneur. She thrives on challenges and new projects.

A native of Pensacola, Florida, she now lives in College Park, Georgia, with her husband, John, who retired after a career in the United States Air Force. They have operated a communications construction company for 15 years. They have two daughters.

She also managed to create the concept for the Puffin' Muffin shops and operates two shops with her partner.

Beverly is interested in raising scholarship money for needy students.

Alice Chapin

Alice Chapin is the author of ten books, but this is the first cookbook project for which she did the writing. An avid baker, she fills her home with the fresh-baked fragrances of breads, cookies, and muffins, often from her own recipes.

A native of Batavia, New York, she now lives in Newnan, Georgia, with her pastor-counselor husband, Norman. They have been on the staff of Campus Crusade for Christ International, Military Ministry for several years as inspirational seminar leaders and speakers. They have four daughters.

Alice has taught elementary school and is a contributor to several magazines in addition to writing her books. Her book *400 Ways to Say "I Love You"* has sold nearly a quarter million copies.